Officer Candidate Guide

Officer Candidate Guide
US Army National Guard

May 2011

Officer Candidate Guide										May 2011

Officer Candidate School, Reserve Component

Summary. This pamphlet provides a guide for US Army National Guard Officer Candidate School students and cadre.

Proponent and exception authority. The proponent of this pamphlet is the Commanding General, US Army Infantry School. The CG, USAIS has the authority to approve exceptions to this pamphlet that are consistent with controlling laws and regulations. The CG, USAIS may delegate this authority, in writing, to a division chief within the proponent agency in the grade of Colonel or the civilian equivalent.

Intent. The intent of this pamphlet is to ensure that National Guard OCS Candidates nationwide share one common standard. It facilitates the cross-state and cross-TASS region boundary training of US Army officer candidates.

Use of the term "States". Unless otherwise stated, whenever the term "States" is used, it is referring to the CONUS States, Alaska, Hawaii, the US Virgin Islands, Territory of Guam, the Commonwealth of Puerto Rico, and District of Columbia.

Supplementation. Local OCS programs may supplement this document in order to meet the needs of local SOPs and regulations, but they may not substantially modify any policy set forth in this document without written authorization from the proponent.

Suggested improvements. Users are invited to send comments and suggested improvements on DA Form 2028 (Recommended Changes to Publications and Blank Forms) directly to the OCS SME, 200th Regiment, Fort McClellan, Alabama 36205.

Distribution. This publication is available in electronic media only and is intended for all Reserve Component OCS cadre and students.

* This pamphlet supersedes all Federal and ARNG Student Guides dated prior to 1 May 2008

Officer Candidate Guide   May 2011

TABLE OF CONTENTS

CHAPTER 1 - ORIENTATION

PARAGRAPH		PAGE
1-1	Gender Statement	1
1-2	Applicability	1
1-3	Mission	1
1-4	Course Overview	1
1-5	Course Standards	1
1-6	Requirements for Graduation with Honors	2
1-7	Student Honors	2
1-8	Definitions	2

CHAPTER 2 – POLICIES

PARAGRAPH		PAGE
2-1	General	4
2-2	Fraternization	4
2-3	Appearance	4
2-4	Candidate Preparation	4
2-5	Contraband	6
2-6	Religious Practices	6
2-7	Leaving the Company Area	6
2-8	Privately Owned Vehicle	6
2-9	Privately Owned Weapons	6

CHAPTER 3 – PROCEDURES

PARAGRAPH		PAGE
3-1	Titles	7
3-2	Saluting, Addressing and Courtesies	7
3-3	Enter as Room / Addressing & Reporting	7
3-4	Making Way and Passing	8
3-5	Movement	8
3-6	Platoon Trainer "Shack" Procedures	9
3-7	Dining Facility Procedures	9
3-8	Sick Call	9
3-9	Classroom Procedures	9
3-10	Formations	9
3-11	Accountability and Reporting	9
3-12	Miscellaneous Rules	9
3-13	Mail	9

CHAPTER 4 – HONOR CODE

PARAGRAPH		PAGE
4-1	General	10
4-2	Provisions of the Honor Code	10
4-3	Honor Council	11

Officer Candidate Guide   May 2011

CHAPTER 5 – CANDIDTE RELIEF, RECYCLE, RESIGNATION		
PARAGRAPH		**PAGE**
5-1	Purpose	12
5-2	Scope	12
5-3	Definitions	12
5-4	Approval Authority	12
5-5	Removing Soldiers from POI Training	12
5-6	Recommendation/Procedures for Recycle and Relief	13
5-7	Candidate Resignations	15
5-8	Candidate Rights	16
CHAPTER 6 – LEADERSHIP RATINGS & REPORTS		
PARAGRAPH		**PAGE**
6-1	General	18
6-2	Evaluation Tools	18
6-3	Leadership Counseling	19
6-4	Army Values	20
6-5	Core Leader competencies	20
6-6	Leadership Attributes	22
6-7	Leadership Positions	23
6-8	Leadership Evaluations	23
CHAPTER 7 – ORGANIZATION OF CANDIDATE COMPANIES		
PARAGRAPH		**PAGE**
7-1	General	25
7-2	Duties of the Chain of Command	25
7-3	Using the Chain of Command	28
7-4	Five Paragraph Operations Order	29
CHAPTER 8 – TRAINING		
PARAGRAPH		**PAGE**
8-1	Pre-OCS Requirements	31
8-2	Phase I Requirements	31
8-3	Phase II Requirements	31
8-4	Phase III Requirements	32
CHAPTER 9 – REQUIRED KNOWLEDGE		
PARAGRAPH		**PAGE**
9-1	Requirements	33
APPENDIX A – PACKING LIST		
PARAGRAPH		**PAGE**
	Insert locally	A-1
APPENDIX B – CANDIDATE AUTOBIOGRAPHY		
PARAGRAPH		**PAGE**

	B-1	Subject Area	B-1
	B-2	Assignment	B-1
	B-3	Assignment Information	B-1
	B-4	Cover Sheet Format	B-2

APPENDIX C – CLOTHING & EQUIPMENT DISPLAYS		
PARAGRAPH		**PAGE**
	Insert Locally	C-1

APPENDIX D – CONTRABAND		
PARAGRAPH		**PAGE**
D-1	Contraband	D-1

APPENDIX E – SENIOR STATUS		
PARAGRAPH		**PAGE**
E-1	General	E-1
E-2	Senior Candidate Uniform	E-1
E-3	Senior Candidate Privileges	E-1

APPENDIX F–	**SAFETY AND COMPOSITE RISK MANAGEMENT**	
F-1	Purpose	F-1
F-2	The Three Tiers of Safety	F-2
F-3	The Risk Management Process	F-2
F-4	Forms	F-2

Officer Candidate Guide   May 2011

Chapter 1
ORIENTATION

1-1. Gender Statement. All references to the male gender throughout this document apply to both sexes unless otherwise indicated.

1-2. Applicability. This guide applies to all candidates assigned to or attached to Reserve Component Officer Candidate School.

1-3. Mission. Train selected personnel in the fundamentals of leadership and basic military skills; instill the professional and physical fitness ethic; evaluate leadership potential; and commission those who qualify as second lieutenants in the Total Force.

1-4. Course Overview.

    a. General: Reserve Component OCS is a 12- to 15-month (traditional program) or 8-week (accelerated program) Leaders' Course of Instruction, taught in a high-stress environment, during which the cadre develop and evaluate the performance of the candidates as it relates to their potential for commissioning as second lieutenants in the Total Force.

    b. Program of Instruction (POI): United States Army Infantry School (USAIS) prepares, publishes, and distributes the OCS Course Management Plan (CMP) and Program of Instruction (POI). The course of instruction will not exceed 16 months and is presented in three phases. The OCS Battalion or Company Commander directs phase advancement, dependent on class performance.

        (1) Pre-OCS. Although not a formal POI phase, traditional OCS programs typically conduct a three-IDT period Phase 0 program. This phase consists of instruction in basic soldier skills, drill and ceremony, physical training, and administrative preparation. The goal is to prepare prospective candidates to succeed in OCS.

        (2) Phase I. Consists of one 15-day annual training period. Training focuses on the individual, squad and platoon levels. Candidates receive military subject, land navigation, and leadership training under high stress conditions. Candidates in Phase I maintain a climate of strict discipline as the cadre show the candidates OCS standards and then expect the candidates to meet these standards. Candidates train under extremely demanding mental and physical conditions.

        (3) Phase II. In the traditional program, Phase II occurs during IDT weekends, between the first and second annual training periods; in the Accelerated Program, Phase II is a four week ADT period. Phase II is characterized by increased Platoon Trainer officer teaching and a slight reduction in stress producing situations. Training focuses on the individual, squad and platoon levels. During this phase, candidates continue to perfect the skills learned in the basic phase and strive for tactical and small unit leadership skills and confidence. Candidates will assume additional responsibilities designed to refine their leadership skills through additional challenges of maintaining a completely functional student chain of command.

        (4) Phase III. Consists of one 15-day annual training period. Training occurs at individual, squad, and platoon level; with the focus on tactical operations and field leadership. Officer candidates focus on polishing leadership skills. The Platoon Trainer officer role is that of a teacher, mentor and role model. This phase is the final refining of the candidate done by the cadre to ultimately prepare the candidate for the officer environment.

1-5. Course Standards.

    a. The standards required of an Officer Candidate will be of the highest order. Character and integrity must be an inspiration to others and conduct at all times must be above reproach. Personal appearance, military bearing and military courtesy will be of the highest standard at all times.

    b. Officer Candidates must meet the following standards necessary for graduation from OCS.

        (1) ACADEMICS. Pass all examinations. (Chapter 8, Training)

        (2) LEADERSHIP. Serve in various command positions during all phases of training and achieve an overall satisfactory leadership rating. (Chapter 6, Leadership Ratings and Reports)

        (3) MORAL CHARACTER. Each Officer Candidate must have high moral character considered necessary for a commissioned officer. (Chapter 4, Honor Code)

        (4) MEDICAL. Each Officer Candidate must pass a physical examination as prescribed for appointment as an officer in AR 40-501.

Officer Candidate Guide   May 2011

(5). PHYSICAL FITNESS. Each Officer Candidate must score a minimum of 60 points on each event of the Army Physical Fitness Test (APFT) with a minimum total score of 180 points, IAW NGR 600-100 and TC 3-22.20 (Army Physical Fitness). A large portion of the OCS environment is physical conditioning and requires stamina. Each Officer Candidate must participate in scheduled physical training. Candidates must complete all foot marches within prescribed standards. During Phase I candidate will complete a 5 mile foot march. During Phase II candidates must complete a 7, 10 mile foot march and a three mile release run. Candidates who fail to meet the standard will be allowed one retest. (Chapter 5, Relief, Recycle, and Resignation)

(6) WEIGHT STANDARDS. All Officer Candidates must meet the weight standards as published in AR 600-9. (Chapter 5, Relief, Recycle, and Resignation)

(7) ATTENDANCE. Each Officer Candidate is expected to attend ALL training periods. Candidates who miss or cannot actively participate in 12 or more hours of scheduled training may be recommended for recycle. (Chapter 5, Relief, Recycle, and Resignation).

1-6. Requirements for Graduation with Honors.

a. All candidates are encouraged to strive for excellence. The earning of a student honor by a candidate is very prestigious and is indicative of the attainment of excellence throughout the course. The criteria for student honors focus on the "whole person" concept and require the candidate to have excelled in physical fitness, academics and leadership. To be eligible for student honors, candidates must meet all graduation requirements.

b. Officer candidates receive honor awards based on their performance in four major areas of the course: Academics, APFT #2, leadership evaluations, and peer evaluations. Any candidate that failed any of the three major areas and had to retest, excluding leadership evaluations, will not be in the running for an honor award. A 'not satisfactory' on a leadership evaluation does not disqualify a candidate from being considered for honor awards.

1-7. Student Honors.

a. Erickson Trophy Recipient / Distinguished Honor Graduate. This award is given to the top candidate in each OCS class in each state. This award is presented by the authority of the Department of the Army and the Air Force, National Guard Bureau and signifies distinguished leadership and academic ability.

b. Academic There is ten end-of-module exams given in Phases I and II of OCS. These exams are averaged for a total academic average (Note: Only the land navigation overall score is counted for the academic award. If a candidate failed any of the tests and had to retest, then that candidate will not be considered for the academic award.) The average of all ten exams will be the determination for the academic award. Failure in any other event (APFT, foot march, leadership evaluation) does not disqualify a candidate from being eligible for consideration for the academic award.

c. Leadership Excellence Award. This award is presented to the candidate with the highest overall leadership evaluation score. This award signifies the candidate who excelled in the leadership aspect of OCS and is in recognition of their superior leadership abilities.

d. Physical Fitness Award. In determining the physical fitness award winner, the overall average of APFTs taken throughout the course will be considered, and the APFT extended scale will be used. A candidate who fails an APFT, and has to re-test in any of the three foot marches or the three mile release runs will not be considered for the physical fitness award.

e. Other Awards Determined by Each Battalion or State

1-8. Definitions

a. OFFICER CANDIDATE (OC). An Officer Candidate is a selected applicant undergoing intensive military training and evaluation to qualify as an officer in the Army National Guard or the US Army Reserve. The standards required to qualify any candidate as an officer regardless of anticipated branch assignment are those prescribed for an Infantry Second Lieutenant. Students enrolled in OCS will be referred to as "Officer Candidate".

b. Platoon Trainer Officer. A Platoon Trainer Officer is a selected officer whose primary function is to TEACH, ASSESS and COUNSEL those candidates assigned to him/her in order to maximize the development of their leadership ability. All Platoon Trainer officers, regardless of rank or position, are selected based on knowledge, experience, dedication and the ability to foster and evaluate leadership performance and potential.

c. Candidates may not fully understand the leadership development process until they have gained the perspective of time and experience. Some of the methods Platoon Trainer Officers use in the performance of their duties are:

1. Observation
2. On-the-spot correction
3. Company/Platoon address
4. Formal instruction
5. Reprimand
6. Informal individual performance counseling
7. Formal individual performance counseling
8. Written evaluation reports
9. Written leadership evaluations
10. Peer reports

c. Platoon Trainer NCO. The Platoon Trainer NCO is generally assigned at the platoon level. A Platoon Trainer NCO is a selected NCO whose primary function is to TEACH, ASSESS and COUNSEL those candidates assigned to him/her in order to maximize the development of their leadership ability. The NCO is an essential component in the command structure of the Army. In the OCS environment, the Platoon Trainer NCO works directly with the Platoon Trainer Officer and in his/her absence takes charge of the platoon. The Platoon Trainer NCO assists in planning and executing platoon missions and trains the platoon in individual and collective tasks. The methods Platoon Trainer NCOs use in the performance of their duties are the same listed above for the Platoon Trainer Officer.

d. SENIOR Platoon Trainer Officer. The senior Platoon Trainer Officer will monitor and supervise leadership training of the candidates and still have the overall responsibility for leadership development and administrative affairs.

Officer Candidate Guide   May 2011

Chapter 2
POLICIES

2-1. General. The policies established at OCS provide uniformity and information for evaluating the candidate's ability to follow instructions, pay attention to detail and demonstrate leadership. The policies prescribed require strict compliance. Failure to comply may result in disciplinary action, recycle or relief.

2-2. Fraternization.

a. Relationships between candidates and cadre which cause the actual or perceived appearance of preferential treatment or partiality are prejudicial to good order, discipline and unit morale. Candidates and cadre are not authorized to form such relationships.

b. Fraternization includes, but is not limited to sexual relationship with candidates and cadre, public display of affection, to include close dancing, handholding, touching, kissing or other similar contact.

c. Fraternization between candidates is unacceptable; it has the potential to undermine unit esprit and cause unnecessary tension within the class. Candidates will refrain from all actions that are, or could be perceived as, fraternization.

2-3. Appearance.

a. An Officer Candidates appearance makes a statement about the individual's personal organization, pride and attention to detail. Officer Candidates will maintain the highest standards of appearance and always set a positive example. Wear and appearance of Army uniforms will be in strict accordance with AR 670-1, except where specific changes are outlined in this candidate guide.

b. Uniforms. Keep all uniforms clean and neat in appearance. Keep boots clean at all times. Wear identification tags at all times. Carry your military identification card with all uniforms except the physical training uniform.

c. Hair.

(1) Male Candidates must wear their hair IAW AR 670-1. Extreme, fad style haircuts or hairstyles are not authorized. Hairstyles that prevent the uniform headgear or protective mask from being worn properly are not authorized. Male Officer Candidates are to be clean-shaven; mustaches and sideburns are not authorized.

(2) Female Candidates: Time allowed for grooming is very limited at OCS. Females should arrive with a hairstyle that conforms to AR 670-1 even during physical training. Hairstyles will not interfere with the proper wearing of military headgear or protective masks. Hair holding ornaments (such as but not limited to, barrettes, pins, clips, bands) if used, must be unadorned and plain and must be transparent or similar in color to the hair, and will be inconspicuously placed. Candidates are not authorized to wear cosmetics.

d. Civilian Clothing. Candidates will wear civilian clothing only at the direction of the OCS Company Commander. When in civilian attire, candidates will conform to the same appearance standards previously prescribed.

2-4. Candidate Preparation

a. Drill and Ceremonies. Candidates must study and become thoroughly familiar with FM 3-21.5 (Drill and Ceremonies). One reading of the FM 3-21.5 will not suffice. A sound, thorough knowledge of Drill and Ceremonies will be of great value to the Officer Candidate. * Specific attention should be paid to chapters 2 through 7 *

b. Physical Fitness. The intent of the physical fitness training program at OCS is to educate each OC on the basics of individual and unit physical fitness and improve the physical fitness of each candidate. It emphasizes running, tactical road marching, endurance, and upper body strength. As future leaders, Officer Candidates are expected to wholeheartedly embrace and exemplify the Army concept of Total Fitness as set forth in TC 3-22.20 and related publications. Physical fitness has a direct impact on combat readiness. With this in mind, the following must be accomplished prior to Phase I:

(1) Acquire a proper pair of running shoes.

(2) Pass the Army Physical Fitness test (APFT) given by the parent RTI/OCS Battalion/OCS Company within 60 days preceding Phase I.

(3) Arrive properly conditioned and capable of moving at the double time for extended distances.

The objectives of the OCS Physical Fitness Program are:

    (1) Teach OCs the basics of physical fitness.

    (2) Teach OCs the proper method of conducting physical fitness. Through study of TC 3-22.20 be prepared to lead warm-up exercises and calisthenics.

    (3) Assist the OCs in achieving and maintaining a high level of physical fitness.

    (4) Develop esprit-de-corps/unit cohesion.

c. Academics. Officer Candidates should review the following references prior to arriving at Phase 1:

    (1) Drill and Ceremonies (FM 3-21.5)

    (2) Army Physical Readiness Training (TC 3-22.20)

    (3) Map Reading and Land Navigation (FM 3-25.26)

    (4) Training Units and Developing Leaders for Full Spectrum Operations (FM 7-0)

    (5) Army Leadership (FM 6-22)

d. Clothing and Equipment. An Officer Candidate's appearance makes a statement about the individual's personal organization, pride and attention to detail. In observance of that fact, Officer Candidates will maintain the highest possible standard of appearance through proper wear and care of the appropriate uniform. In addition to this, all Officer Candidates will be uniformly dressed for whatever task or situation that they are in.

    (1) It is the Officer Candidate's responsibility to make sure that he has in his possession all authorized and required items. Diligence and persistence are often necessary. If after every effort to acquire the necessary clothing and equipment from your home unit is unsuccessful, contact the respective Regional Training Institute (RTI) for guidance and assistance.

    (2) Boots. **Boots must be broken in thoroughly before beginning OCS.**

        1. Blisters and related foot problems will cause candidates to miss training. If this occurs, it will be directly attributable to failure to prepare.

        2. Boots are expected to be clean and maintained with an appropriate suede cleaning kit.

        3. Trousers will be bloused unless otherwise directed.

e. Uniforms. There is only one type of uniform required for Phase 1.

    (1) ACU minimum 5 sets. Uniform items will not be mixed. Each student must acquire and maintain the high standards of personal appearance of the officer corps. It is expected that the Officer Candidate will set his uniform standard for the remaining years of their career. Those students who have uniforms that show considerable wear or that are ill-fitting will correct those deficiencies prior to reporting to Phase I.

        a. Embroidered nametapes and U.S. Army tape will be IAW AR 670-1, Paragraph 28-22.

        b. Officer Candidates will not wear ribbons, awards, decorations, unit patches, U.S. flag, combat patches, or other insignia upon reporting to Phase I. Subsequent wear of ribbons, awards, decorations and unit patches, U.S. flag, combat patches, and other insignia will be permitted at the discretion of the SR Platoon Trainer.

        c. Candidates will wear their uniforms as prescribed in AR 670-1 and the directives of the OCS Battalion.

    (2) Physical Fitness Uniform (PT), minimum 2 sets.

        a. Improved Physical Fitness Uniform (IPFU).

        b. Plain white socks will be worn with the top above the ankle but below the calf.

        c. One pair of running shoes as preferred by the Officer Candidate that are of subdued colors and appropriate for soldiers.

f. Equipment.

(1) The Kevlar helmet is the prescribed headgear for OCS, unless stated otherwise. The helmet is worn with the chinstrap fitting snugly on the chin. Officer Candidates are required to have a soft cap in their possession at all times.

(2). Load bearing equipment (LBE) will be worn IAW Appendix C. The poncho will be neatly folded and secured to the rear of the pistol belt on the LBE, IAW Appendix C. Excess straps on the LBE will be folded up toward the adjustment buckle in a 1-inch fold and secured with green tape. LBE may be substituted by the LBV.

(3) Two canteens will be worn on the pistol belt over the hip pockets. Canteens will be full when LBE is worn, empty while in wall locker. Canteen cup will be carried inside the canteen cover.

g. Clothing and Equipment Displays: All clothing and equipment will be displayed IAW OC Guide. All displays will be uniform throughout the Officer Candidate Company.

2-5. Contraband. Contraband is defined as any item that is destructive to the good order and discipline, health, welfare, or safety of the soldier or unit. The Company Commander must approve all over-the-counter medicine. See Appendix D for contraband list.

2-6. Religious Practices.

a. Candidates will have an opportunity to participate in religious activities when possible. Religious activities will be IAW local SOP.

b. Accommodating religious practices. A candidate may submit a written request for accommodation of a religious practice(s) to the Company Commander for consideration.

2-7. Leaving the Company Area.

a. When leaving the company area (i.e. sick call, etc.), candidates sign out IAW local SOP.

b. The Company or Battalion Commander is the only one who may excuse a candidate from a scheduled class.

c. The Company Commander, First Sergeant, or Senior Platoon Trainer are the only ones who can grant permission for a candidate to leave the company area.

2-8. Privately Owned Vehicles. Refer to local SOP.

2-9. Privately Owned Weapons (POWs).

a. There isn't any place for POWs or Law Enforcement weapons in OCS training. Address regulatory concerns IAW unit SOP through the chain of command.

b. The carrying or possession of the following weapons is prohibited: unregistered firearms or pellet guns, switchblade knives, knives with fixed blades, knives with blades in excess of three inches in length, brass knuckles, leaded canes, gas dispensers, starter pistols, explosive devices (to include ammunition), projectiles, num-chucks, devices designed or altered to permit its use as an unregistered weapon, blackjacks, rappers, raps, or other related devices, and pyrotechnics of any type for other than authorized use.

c. Candidates will turn in any unauthorized weapon IAW local SOP.

Officer Candidate Guide   May 2011

Chapter 3
POLICIES

3-1. Titles. Candidates will be identified by the title of "Officer Candidate [Last Name]. Senior Officer Candidates will be addressed as "Senior Officer Candidate [Last Name}

3-2. Saluting, Addressing and Courtesies.

    a. Saluting. Salutes will be rendered IAW FM 3-21.5 (Drill and Ceremonies). To further emphasize saluting, attention to detail, and being cognizant of ones surroundings, saluting distance will be that distance at which a candidate recognizes an officer.

    b. When addressed by an officer, a candidate stands at the position of attention. Candidates reply, "Sir, Officer Candidate [Last Name]." When addressed by an NCO, candidates will stand at parade rest and respond, "Sergeant, Officer Candidate [Last Name]." When addressing either an officer or NCO, the candidate will look directly into the eyes of the officer or NCO he is addressing.

    c. Greetings. An appropriate greeting will be extended when saluting (i.e. "Sir, Officer Candidate, *name*, Good Morning, Sir!"). When in groups of two or more, the Officer Candidate in charge will call the group to attention and render the salute and proper greeting. The Officer Candidate greeting the officer will continue to do so until the salute has been returned, the command "Carry On" has been given, or the officer is no longer in view. When moving as a group the first Officer Candidate in file or the Officer Candidate in charge will greet the officer. Greetings will not be extended at the double time. Candidate in charge will slow to quick time; render the salute and proper greeting (without stopping forward motion), and return to double time after the salute is returned.

        (1) When addressing groups of officers and/or NCOs only the senior member of the group shall be addressed.

        (2) If the senior member of the addressed group is accompanied by a member of equal grade then the senior members will be addressed as Gentlemen, Ladies, or Ma'am/Sir as appropriate.

        (3) Proper greetings are determined by local time.

            a. Morning is from 0001 to 1159.

            b. Afternoon is from 1200 to 1759.

            c. Evening is from 1800 to 2400.

            d. All greetings are concluded with Sir/Ma'am as appropriate.

    d. When initiating conversation with cadre, candidates must "Request permission to speak." This is not required when saluting or rendering military courtesies.

    e. During duty hours, when an officer enters the company area/barracks, the first candidate to see the officer will command, "Company/Platoon/Squad/Group, Attention." Conversely, if any NCO without an officer present enters the area, the area will be called "At ease." All candidates who hear the command will respond appropriately. When the officer/NCO replies "Carry on" candidates will continue their activities.

    f. When an officer or NCO enters the platoon area the first candidate to see him will call "Attention" for an officer and "At ease" for a NCO. The nearest platoon leader or platoon sergeant will report to the officer/NCO with the platoon status.

3-3. Enter a Room, Addressing/Reporting Dismissing.

    a. Enter a room. Candidates will assume the position of attention, center themselves in the doorway and toe the line (the line is the imaginary line between the center of the doorframe, parallel to the doorway), knock three times with the palm of the right hand on the right door frame. The candidate will wait till the person in the room addresses the officer candidate, then the candidate will announce "Sir/Ma'am [as appropriate], Officer Candidate [Last Name] requests permission to enter." The candidate will wait at the position of attention until told to enter. Once told to enter, the candidate will enter and walk directly to a position of two steps and centered in front of the desk (or officer's location), assume the position of attention, and simultaneously render the hand salute while saying, "Sir/Ma'am, Officer Candidate [Last Name] reports as ordered / with a question / with a statement" The candidate will execute order arms when the officer returns the salute.

Officer Candidate Guide   May 2011

b. Addressing/Reporting

(1) To a commissioned officer: When addressed by an officer the Officer Candidate will come to the position of attention and state his name as follows, "Sir/Ma'am, Officer Candidate *name* reports with a statement/question/as ordered". During the conversation, the Officer Candidate will preface any comment, answer or reply with "Sir/Ma'am, Officer Candidate *name*". The comment, answer, reply will not conclude with Sir/Ma'am unless the reply is "Yes" or "No" or is otherwise directed in this guide. When reporting to an officer the Officer Candidate will come to the position of attention, render a salute and report, "Sir/Ma'am Officer Candidate *name*, reports!" If the Officer Candidate has been ordered to report, the candidate will add, "As ordered!"

(2) To a non-commissioned officer: Same as above with the exception of the hand salute and Officer Candidates will use the term "Sergeant" or "Sergeant Major" instead of "Sir/Ma'am".

c. Dismissing.

(1) From a commissioned officer: When the conversation is complete and the Officer Candidate is dismissed, the Officer Candidate will come to the position of attention, take one step to the rear with the left foot, render the salute, extend the greeting of the day "Sir/Ma'am Officer Candidate *name*. Good Morning / Afternoon / Evening, Sir/Ma'am!" After the salute has been returned the OC will execute an about face and exit.

(2) From a non-commissioned officer: Same as above with the exception of the salute and Officer Candidates will use the term "Sergeant" or Sergeant Major" instead of "Sir/Ma'am".

3-4. Making Way and Passing.

a. Making Way. When cadre enter a hallway or stairwell and are six steps away, candidates will assume the position of attention, with the shoulders, buttocks and heels touching the wall and command, "Make way." (All candidates will echo this command). Candidates will resume their activities on the command of "Carry on." (All Candidates will echo this command). If the cadre does not command "Carry on," one of the candidates will give the command after the cadre has passed beyond six steps.

b. Requesting Permission to Pass. Whenever an officer's or NCO's presence impedes normal traffic and a candidate desires to pass, the candidate comes to the position of attention facing the officer or NCO and says, "[Title], Officer Candidate [Last Name] requests permission to pass." When permission is granted, the candidate will pass. If a group of officers or NCOs are present the candidate requests permission to pass from the ranking individual.

3-5. Movement.

a. Marching in formation.

(1) Three or more candidates constitute a formation. Formations will march in columns when six (6) or fewer candidates are present; will march two (2) abreast when the formation contains between seven (7) and eleven (11) candidates; will march three abreast when the formation contains 12 or more candidates. Candidates march no more than two abreast on footpaths or sidewalks.

(2) Formations will not depart a training location without ensuring proper accountability. The class will carry the class guidon whenever they march. Display the guidon, when not in use, in the unit area. In order to secure the guidon the "Key" must be removed. The guidon bearer shall not surrender the guidon and guidon key to anyone unless directed to do so by the Senior Platoon Trainer, Platoon Trainer Company Commander, or Platoon Trainer First Sergeant.

(3) Candidates in groups of three or more will move in formation with a member in charge.

b. Road Guards. Road guards are required for all company formation movements. Road guards wear the road guard vest during all formation movements. During hours of twilight or darkness, road guards carry an operational flashlight in the hand closest to the outside of the formation. Road guard responsibilities are:

(1) Front road guards will lead the element by 30 feet and rear road guards will trail the element by 30 feet. During periods of limited visibility road guards increase the distance to 50 feet.

(2) Front and rear road guards warn traffic of the formation. They do not post themselves at an intersection that is the responsibility of the formation internal road guards.

(3) Formation internal road guards will post at each intersection and maintain that position until relieved or the element has passed.

Officer Candidate Guide   May 2011

(4) Road guards that are posting at intersections will stand at a modified position of parade rest. Their right arm will be extended in front of their body warning the oncoming traffic to stop. Once relieved or the formation has passed, the road guard will come to the position of attention and move back to the formation.

(5) Road guards will come to the position of attention and salute any vehicle displaying a blue Department of Defense vehicle registration sticker, as well as any vehicle displaying General Officer or VIP plates.

3-6. "Platoon Trainer Shack" Procedures. *Insert local procedures*

3-7. Dining Facility Procedures. *Insert local procedures*

3-8. Sick Call. *Insert local procedures*

3-9. Classroom Procedures. *Insert local procedures*

3-10. Formations.

a. Scheduled formations are listed on the training schedule and/or drill period operations order. The cadre chain of command may call other formations. Candidates are considered late to formation if they are not standing in their platoon when the command "Fall-in" is given. Candidates will not miss formation unless excused by their Platoon Trainer.

b. The student chain of command is responsible for accountability of the company.

c. Candidates are responsible for knowing the time of the next scheduled formation prior to departing the training site on an IDT weekend.

3-11. Accountability and Reporting.

a. The student chain of command is responsible for accounting for all students assigned to their company/platoon. Accountability and reporting procedures are IAW FM 3-21.5

3-12. Miscellaneous Rules.

a. All areas not specifically authorized by OCS cadre are off limits to Officer Candidates.

b. Officer Candidates will not swear, cuss, or use abusive language at anytime.

c. Vending areas and telephones are off limits unless otherwise directed by the Platoon Trainer Staff.

d. Officer Candidates will double-time at all times except:

(1) When otherwise directed.

(2) Immediately after meals.

(3) When carrying large or unwieldy objects.

(4) When on profile.

(5) Upon reaching Senior Status, time permitting.

e. Officer Candidates may wear a wedding ring on the left hand and a wristwatch. No other jewelry is authorized to include earrings and other body piercings. Candidates will make certain all alarms and chimes on watches are "OFF" prior to the start of the day's activities.

3-13. Mail.

a. See your OCS Company's local SOP or the addendum to this chapter for information on mail collection/mail call. Mail will never be withheld as a form of punishment.

b. Packages. All candidates receiving packages will notify their Platoon Trainer. Candidates cannot accept "care packages" containing contraband or perishable items until authorized by the Company Commander. All packages are subject to inspection upon receipt.

Officer Candidate Guide   May 2011

Chapter 4
HONOR CODE

4-1. General.

    a. Honor.

        (1) Honor may be defined as that quality in a person that shows them to be truthful and fair in word and deed, both to themselves and to others. It also implies loyalty, courage and devotion to duty.

        (2) A commissioned officer must possess honor as an integral portion of his character in order to meet the demands placed upon him as a leader. In the profession of arms, the welfare and indeed the very lives of so many, hinge on the honor and integrity of the few who lead. You will be among those few. In peacetime, it is imperative that you maintain your high standards of honor so that in combat, the trust placed in you will not be misplaced.

        (3) The honor code takes a simplistic approach to govern the behavior of Officer Candidates in a complex environment. The honor code simply holds the Officer Candidate to conduct that our society deems acceptable and honorable; the conduct primarily learned at home, school and church. The honor code to be effective must be monitored and sanctioned by the Officer Candidates.

    b. Webster's Definition of Honor.

        "...a sense of what is right, just and true, scorning meanness." Honor, like courage, is a word, which has resisted thorough definition, though such has been attempted by the philosophers of the ancient world and perhaps by aspiring officers caught in situations of compromise. Honor encompasses all of the acts, thoughts and aspirations of an individual. Its presence or absence in the personal make-up of an individual determines how he lives, what he derives from life and how he is thought of by others.

    c. A leader must have the respect of those persons given into his charge. This respect is based upon his conduct, his personal courage and his sense of honor. Honor is, therefore, a necessary and essential part of every officer. He is bound by his word, his devotion to Duty, Honor, Country and the oath of his commission. In times of war and peace, his word will invariably be given in times of extreme tension, stress and danger. His subordinates depend on this word for their physical survival and his superior depends on it in shaping the plans of battle. Honor among soldiers, invariably, makes the difference between life and death.

4-2. Provisions of the Honor Code. The honor code is simple: ***An Officer Candidate will not lie, cheat, or steal, nor tolerate those who do***.

    a. The Honor Code is a rule of personal integrity, which requires each student to be absolutely and unfailingly honest in all matters. The code at Officer Candidate School is as follows: "Belief in and application of the principles of the Honor Code will set the standard for and influence everything you do! Never fear the truth and never compromise honor or truth for expediency."

    b. The element most important to the success of the Honor Code is the belief in that code by every person. That belief, together with an appreciation for the importance of honor, will foster the assurance that you can put complete trust in your comrades. Honor and trust are the cohesive agents, which transform a group into a unit.

    c. The Honor Code is based on the principle that integrity is an essential attribute for all officers. At OCS, the Honor Code is emphasized and candidates must understand its scope and intent. Each candidate must employ it in everything they do.

        (1) **Lying**. Candidates violate the honor code by lying if they make an oral or written statement or gesture of communication in the presence of, or to, another, intending to deceive or mislead. Quibbling is creation of false impressions through evasive wording, the omission of relevant facts, or telling a partial truth, and is a form of lying.

        (2) **Cheating**. Candidates violate the honor code by cheating if they willingly take information, which does not belong to them, or present material that is not an example of their own work, to gain an advantage.

        (3) **Stealing**. Candidates violate the honor code by stealing if they wrongfully take, obtain, or withhold, by any means, from the possession of the owner (or any other person), any money, personal property or article of value of any kind, with the intent to deprive or defraud another person of the use or benefit of the property. Candidates are considered to be stealing when they take, obtain, or withhold any item without the expressed permission or knowledge of the owner.

(4) **Toleration**. Candidates violate the honor code by toleration if they fail to report an unresolved incident with honor implications to the proper authority within a reasonable time period. Proper authority will usually be the Platoon, Platoon Trainer or an honor council representative; however, an incident could also be reported to an instructor or member of the support staff. A reasonable length of time is the time it takes to confront the suspected violator and determine whether the incident was a misunderstanding or actually a violation of the honor code.

   d. There is a distinct difference between an honor violation and a disciplinary violation. Although honor and discipline are in many ways complimentary, it is essential that the Officer Candidate completely understand the difference. To be guilty of an Honor Code Violation, you must have violated one of the four provisions of the Honor Code. A disciplinary violation involves a breach of policy or regulations.

4-3. The Honor Council.

   a. The honor council investigates and makes recommendations to the OCS Battalion Commander with regard to any alleged or actual violations of the honor code. The honor council consists of four elements: the Senior Platoon Trainer Officer, at a minimum of two Officer Candidates (usually the president and vice president), at least two other cadre or staff members and a recorder.

   b. Senior Platoon Trainer. The duties of the Senior Platoon Trainer will include providing direction and advice to the honor council. The Senior Platoon Trainer will not vote unless there is a tie among the other council members. He will notify the OCS Battalion Commander of the results of all hearing and recommend retention or relief of the candidate(s) involved.

   c. Investigations. A preliminary investigation of alleged violations is conducted by the SR Platoon Trainer during Phase I, Phase II and Phase III. Every fact of the alleged violation is explored. Written statements must be obtained from the principle witnesses.

   (1). An example of an investigation is as follows. OC Doe is seen apparently cheating during an exam. The instructor informs the Senior Platoon Trainer that this occurs. The Senior Platoon Trainer conducts the investigation, by speaking with the individual, and other classmates. If there is sufficient evidence, the Senior Platoon Trainer then convenes an Honor Council.

   (2) Prior to the hearing, the SR Platoon Trainer council informs the alleged violator of the following:

   a. He is bound by the honor code to tell the truth.

   b. The charges relating to the violation and the identity of the accuser.

   c. He may bring in any evidence, or call on any witness, on his behalf.

   d. He may make an oral or written statement.

   e. He has the right to be represented by another candidate.

   d. Conduct of the Hearing. Normally, the hearing is conducted within 24 hours. The Senior Platoon Trainer will determine if all procedural items have been accomplished and the accused is prepared to plead their case. The following are the rules and procedures for the hearing:

   (1) The SR Platoon Trainer presents the case to the committee. There must be at least three committee members present at the hearing.

   (2) The violator and accuser will not be present in the hearing at the same time.

   (3) The Senior Platoon Trainer is present throughout the entire hearing. Alleged violators are considered not guilty until proven otherwise. A majority of votes cast in secret ballot, will be required to find a candidate guilty of an honor code violation.

   (4). Staff or Candidates who have been part of the investigation or who are biased in any way will not sit on the council and the Senior Platoon Trainer will select another member.

   (5) A candidate found guilty of an honor code violation is recommended by the council for dismissal from the OCS program. The verdict and recommendation of an Honor Board will be forwarded to the OCS / GS Battalion Commander. If the OC is found not guilty, the verdict is forwarded through the OCS / GS Battalion Commander as part of the minutes of the meeting. The OCS / GS Battalion Commander will make final decision for candidate disposition after looking at the facts and the Honor Councils recommendation.

A VIOLATION OF THE HONOR CODE IS CAUSE FOR DISMISSAL!

Officer Candidate Guide			May 2011
Chapter 5

Chapter 5. OFFICER CANDIDATE RELIEF, RECYCLE, AND RESIGNATION

5-1. Purpose: This chapter prescribes the policies and procedures for the relief or recycle of an officer candidate in the OCS program and provisions for the relief/dismissal of officer candidates from training.

5-2. Scope: These policies and procedures apply to all officer candidates in the ARNG OCS program during all phases of training, both traditional and accelerated.

5-3. Definitions: The ARNG OCS program provides two official remedies for soldiers who do not meet course requirements, require disciplinary action, or cannot successfully continue OCS training. Commanders at all levels are not restricted to these remedies and may provide remedies as the situation dictates with the means available; however, these remedies are provided. Candidates relieved/dismissed, and resignations from the OCS program will be administratively reduced to the rank held prior to enrollment in OCS within one month. Date of Rank (DOR) will be the DOR held prior to enrollment to OCS.

   a. **Relief from current phase of training:** This is the relief/dismissal of an officer candidate from the current phase of training they are in for one of the reasons outlined in paragraph 5-6 i. The candidate is returned to their home state/unit of assignment for further action on relief from the OCS program or to be recycled.

   b. **Relief from OCS Program:** This occurs when a candidate is relieved/dismissed from the current phase of training and returns to their home state. The OCS company commander at their home state recommends relief from the OCS program to the GS/OCS Battalion Commander for approval.

   c. **Recycle:** Recycle occurs when an officer candidate is relieved/dismissed from the current phase of training and returns to their home state/unit. The home state is responsible for determining if the candidate is to be recycled. If the candidate is recycled, he/she must start at the beginning of the phase in which they were relieved/dismissed. If the candidate is not recycled, he/she will be administratively reduced IAW the provisions specified in paragraph 5-3 above.

   d. **Resignation.** Resignation occurs when an officer candidate resolves to leave OCS training, submits this request in writing, and is granted this request by the commander.

5-4. Approval Authority. OCS Battalion and OCS Companies in each State will develop and implement a detailed local SOP for relief and recycle IAW AR 350-1 and provisions of the OCS CMP.

   a. Accelerated and Consolidated Phase I and III. The OCS Battalion Commander at an Accelerated (all phases) or Consolidate phase I and III has the authority to relieve soldiers from the current phase of training for which they supervise if the soldier fails to meet any of the reasons listed in 5-6i of this guide.

   b. The authority to relieve or recycle a soldier from the ARNG OCS program resides in the soldier's home state only. Soldiers may only be relieved from or recycled in the OCS program by the authority of the first O5 in the candidate's chain of command (OCS Battalion Commander or GS Battalion/RTI Commander) in the officer candidate's home state. If the decision to relieve a candidate is made, the commander must determine if the soldier is to be relieved with prejudice or without prejudice.

   (1) Relief without prejudice. IAW AR 350-1, disenrollment for illness, injury, or other reasons beyond the control of the individual will be made without prejudice. This type of relief allows the soldier the option of reapplying for a future class enrollment.

   (2) Relief with prejudice. Occurs when in the opinion of the approval authority (described in Paragraph 5-4, b. above), the soldier should be removed from the ARNG OCS program without the option to reapply for a future class enrollment. This is normally reserved for serious, involuntary reasons for relief.

5-5. Removing Soldiers from POI Training. The only person authorized to remove an officer candidate from training is the approval authority (described in Paragraph 5-4). Officer candidates continue to attend all POI training until final disposition on relief, recycle or appeal is determined. The approval authority may remove officer candidates from POI training before final disposition if they determine that the officer candidate's presence

Officer Candidate Guide   May 2011

constitutes a significant training distracter for other candidates or constitutes a safety hazard to other candidates or cadre. However, if an OC appeals and appeal is favored to the OC and they are allowed to continue in the OCS program, the responsible OCS commander must provide OC with all missed/make-up training.

5-6. Recommendations/Procedures for Relief or Recycle.

  a. Responsibilities.

   (1) Platoon Trainer. The candidate must first be counseled in writing (DA Form 4856) that he/she is in jeopardy of being relieved or recycled. The counseling must contain the areas in which the candidate must improve, or actions that the candidate must discontinue in order to maintain enrollment in the current class, along with a specified amount of time they have to complete the corrective action. If the candidate does not improve or does not discontinue actions as directed, the Platoon Trainer must counsel the candidate a second time in writing (DA Form 4856) recommending him/her for relief or recycle. At this second counseling session, the Platoon Trainer informs the candidate of their appeal rights, para 5-8. This evidence is included in the candidate's record along with counseling forms concerning the recycle or relief. The Platoon Trainer then presents the OCS company commander with complete documentation and evidence concerning all efforts made on the candidate's behalf.

   (2) Company Commander. The company commander reviews the training packet, interviews the candidate, and concurs or non-concurs with the recommendation. Record of interview will be in writing (using DA Form 4856). If the OCS company commander decides that the candidate's actions do not warrant relief, the documents are maintained in the candidate record and the candidate continues in the OCS course. If the OCS company commander concurs with the recommendation, the packet is forwarded to the OCS Battalion Commander, the GS Battalion/RTI Commander, or the Regimental / Battalion Commander, as appropriate.

   (3) Commander (OCS Battalion, GS Battalion or Regimental). The commander reviews the packet along with the candidate's records, receives input from the candidate's chain of command, and interviews the candidate. The commander can concur or non-concur with the recommendation or take other action as appropriate. The Commander will record his/her recommendation in Part IV of the Company Commander's DA Form 4856.

  b. Dismissal for misconduct, lack of motivation, academic deficiency or failure to maintain physical fitness or height and weight standards will be recorded on the OCs End of Course Summary, if applicable, in accordance with the provisions of this CMP. In accordance with AR 600-8-2, soldiers disenrolled for disciplinary reasons may be flagged. Soldiers disenrolled for misconduct may be barred from reenlistment in accordance with AR 601-280, AR 140-111 and NGR 600-100.

  c. Disenrollment for illness, injury, compassionate transfer or other reasons beyond the control of the individual will be made without prejudice. The O5 commander will prepare a DD Form 785 (Record of Disenrollment for Officer Candidate – Type Training) to the OC's State OCS company/RTI commander stating the reason for termination and that the student will be eligible to re-enroll as soon as conditions that led to disenrollment no longer exist.

  d. The Federal UCMJ and/or UCMJ from one State do not apply to ARNG soldiers under Title 32, U.S. Code from another State. Accordingly school commanders will forward an ARNG soldier's case to Soldier's respective State Adjutant General for appropriate disposition.

  e. School commanders will ensure student records are complete and audit trails are maintained for all personnel actions.

  f. Final Disposition. The candidate packet and recommendation for recycle or relief is then forwarded to the candidate's home state OCS or GS Battalion/RTI commander for disposition.

  g. Records. Records for a candidate being relieved are maintained for 2 years with a DD Form 785, (Record of Disenrollment from Officer Candidate Type Training) at the school relieving the candidate IAW TR PAM 350-18, para. 3-25 b. These records must include a completed "End of Course Summary". Recycled candidate's records are maintained on file until the candidate resumes training at the start of the phase which previously dropped. The candidate record then again becomes the candidate's active record. All documents concerning the recycle are maintained in the candidate's record.

h. Reasons for Recycle. The State Company Commander with approval from the first 05/GS Battalion Commander determines the grounds for recycle. They may include, but are not limited to the following:

(1) Compassionate or hardship reasons. Health, welfare or financial problems of immediate family members that substantially interfere with successful continuation in the course or causes candidates to miss 12 or more hours of scheduled training.

(2) Disqualifying physical conditions (medical). Inability to complete the course because of poor health or missing training through hospitalization, appointments or duty limitations directed by a medical officer. Physical profiles are administered to prevent soldiers from exercising personal zeal beyond their physical limitations. The Company Commander considers a possible recycle for profiles that:

(a) Cause a candidate to limit participation in physical activities, routine duty, or miss excessive amount of scheduled physical training periods.

(b) Require confinement to quarters for a contagious sickness or illness causing the OC to miss 12 or more hours of scheduled training.

(c) Prevent a candidate from participating in mandatory course requirements or miss a portion of critical training. Examples are: Leaders' Reaction Course, APFT, FLX I, II, road marches, physical training runs, and so forth.

(3) Disciplinary reasons. Failure to cooperate in routine requirements or adhere to course standards of obedience. Candidates who receive repeated disciplinary actions are recommended for recycle or relief. Candidates committing any offense punishable by applicable laws and / or military regulations are considered for relief under this provision.

(4) Failed leadership evaluations. Candidates who fail to display improvement in leadership, and who continue to receive sub par leadership evaluations must be considered for relief or recycle. OCS Company Commanders who do not feel that an officer candidate possesses the leadership skills, attitudes, and knowledge to become a successful second lieutenant must prevent the candidate from graduating from Phase II and proceeding to Phase III, and must consider the candidate for recycle or relief.

(5) Failure to progress. Defines a candidate who shows marginal progress in performance, physical fitness, leadership evaluations, demonstrated motivation, attitude, aptitude, and conduct when compared to candidate's peers.

(6) Failure to meet graduation requirements.

i. Reasons for Relief. The OCS Battalion Commander at Consolidated Phase Training or the State OCS BN/GS Battalion Commander determines the grounds for relief. They may include, but are not limited to the following.

(1) Honor Code violations. A candidate will not lie, cheat, steal, nor tolerate those who do. A violation of this code may result in a recommendation for relief. See ARNG OCS Platoon Trainer Guide and ARNG OCS OC Guide for detailed information concerning the honor code.

(2) Academic failure. Academic failure is defined as a failure to attain 70% on any academic evaluations or the scheduled retest.

(3) Failure to progress. This is a candidate who fails to show progress in performance, physical fitness, subjective evaluations, motivation, attitude, aptitude, or conduct. Such progress is less than acceptable and is detrimental to the interest of the other students in the class.

(4) Disciplinary reasons. Failure to cooperate in routine requirements or adhere to course standards of obedience. Candidates who receive repeated disciplinary actions are recommended for recycle or relief. Candidates committing any offense punishable under applicable laws and / or military regulations are considered for relief under this provision.

(5) Failed leadership evaluations. Candidates who fail to display improvement in leadership, and who continue to receive sub par leadership evaluations must be considered for relief or recycle. OCS Company

Officer Candidate Guide   May 2011

Commanders who do not feel that an officer candidate possesses the leadership skills, attitudes and knowledge to become a successful second lieutenant must prevent the candidate from graduating from Phase II and proceeding to Phase III, and must consider the candidate for recycle or relief.

(6) Lack of adaptability. A candidate who fails to adapt to the stringent environmental conditions of discipline, soldierly habits, teamwork, and mental and physical stress can be considered for relief. A candidate who exhibits behavior contradictory to normally expected behavior can be referred to the OCS Company Commander for further evaluation prior to a relief recommendation.

(7) Lack of motivation. Lack of motivation is characterized by a candidate's failure to exert reasonable effort to succeed, constant malingering, or a personal attitude, which demonstrates little or no desire to complete a course of action or mission.

(8) Falsifying or omitting facts or information. Knowingly falsifying or omitting facts concerning enrollment or commissioning requirements or documents.

(9) Misconduct. Misconduct includes but is not limited to:

(a) Candidate / Candidate or Candidate / Cadre fraternization. OCS is a gender-integrated environment and is an intense 24-hour a day course of instruction. Candidate teamwork and loyalty is paramount in the development of leaders. A candidate's actions must be embedded in the Army's core values: loyalty, duty, respect, selfless service, honor, integrity and personal courage. Therefore, candidates do not engage in fraternization. Failure to follow these guidelines may result in relief from the course. Male and female candidates and cadre interact closely with one another and must exercise self-discipline and good judgment to prevent compromising situations. Male and female candidates are not authorized to engage in any real or perceived conduct with one another that is conduct unbecoming of an officer and contrary to accepted Army standards for values, ethics, and the current Code of Conduct. For detailed information on what constitutes fraternization see ARNG OCS Platoon Trainer Guide or ARNG OCS OC Guide.

(b) Unauthorized alcohol use.

(c) Integrity issues.

(d) Possession, use, sale, or transfer of any narcotic, hallucinogen, controlled substance or narcotics paraphernalia.

(e) Conduct that would constitute a violation of applicable laws and / or military regulations and / or the Honor Code.

5-7. Candidate Resignations. Every effort must be made by the ARNG OCS cadre to counsel and advise an individual toward the successful completion of OCS. In cases where these efforts do not prevent an officer candidate from requesting resignation the following procedures are followed.

a. Responsibilities.

(1) Officer candidate. The officer candidate must submit their request for resignation from the ARNG OCS program in writing to the cadre chain of command.

(2) Cadre. The Platoon Trainer counsels the candidate on a DA Form 4856 detailing the procedure for and the consequences of resignation. The Platoon Trainer also submits written comments on the candidate's potential to the company commander, along with the candidate's written resignation and complete candidate record.

(3) Company commander. The company commander interviews the candidate and counsels the candidate on a DA Form 4856 on the consequences of his / her resignation. He/she may add his/her own comments to the Platoon Trainer's written comments on the candidate's potential before forwarding the entire packet to the OCS/GS Battalion or Regimental Commander.

(4) OCS or GS Battalion Commander (approval authority). The Battalion Commander interviews the candidate, counsels the candidate on the consequences of his / her resignation, and accepts the candidates

Officer Candidate Guide   May 2011

resignation if the candidate is determined to resign from the ARNG OCS program. The final decision of the Battalion Commander is recorded on a DA Form 4856 Part IV initiated by the OCS Company Commander.

b. Final Disposition. After the Battalion Commander accepts the officer candidate's resignation, the candidate is removed from training. The Platoon Trainer and the OCS company commander complete the end of course summary and place it in the candidate record.

c. Records. Records are maintained on file at the home state on all officer candidates who resign. These records include the completed end of course summary on the officer candidate.

d. Withdrawing a resignation. If the candidate elects to withdraw the resignation before it is forwarded to the OCS or GS Battalion Commander, the documents are retained in the candidate record with the DA Form 4856 Part IV completed by the Company Commander explaining the candidate's decision. A resignation in lieu of relief is processed as a relief.

5-8. Candidate Rights. The following procedures apply in cases where relief/dismissal is considered for motivational, disciplinary, or academic reasons:

a. IAW AR 350-1 and TR 350-18, The Platoon Trainer will notify the student in writing of the proposed action, the basis for the action, the consequences of disenrollment, and the right to appeal. The Platoon Trainer will advise the student that any appeal must be submitted within 7 duty days after receipt of the written notification of the dismissal action by the Battalion Commander. Appeals will be submitted to the school commandant or commander. The student will acknowledge by written endorsement within 2 duty days receipt of the written notification of dismissal action. The endorsement must indicate whether or not the student intends to appeal the dismissal action.

(1) Appeals will be forwarded to the school commandant or commander who will refer the proposed action and the appeal to the OSJA to determine legal sufficiency of the dismissal decision. All appellate actions will become part of the student's case file. Commandants and commanders will make their final decision on dismissals after considering the supporting OSJA recommendation. In cases where a OSJA is not available, the commandant or commander will forward appeals to the commander who has GCMCA for review and final decision.

(2) Students who elect to appeal will remain actively enrolled in the course pending disposition of their appeals.

(3) All appeals must clearly provide new evidence not previously considered by the Approving Authority.

b. Resign in lieu of relief. Candidates are counseled that resignation is an option but it voids any appellate rights and that it may not necessarily better their chances of returning to OCS.

c. Appeal Packets consist of the appeal consideration memorandum and at a minimum, the following attachments, if applicable. Local OSJA offices may require more documentation.

(1) 3rd party statements

(2) statements from the chain of command

(3) other official documents or evidence

d. Upon receipt of the appeal packet, the RTI Commander ensures the packet is complete and coordinates for OSJA review.

e. The OSJA reviews the appeal packet for legal sufficiency and provides the RTI Commander with their recommendation.

f. The RTI Commander will make the final decision after considering the OSJA's recommendation.

g. The RTI Commander will notify the Approval Authority of the final decision and counsel the candidate of the decision.

h. The decision of the RTI Commander is final.

i. If the candidate wins the appeal they will continue on with training. If the candidate had been removed from training they must be provided a fair opportunity to make up the missed training. The OCS Company Commander and the Sr. Instructor will coordinate the missed training.

j. If the candidate loses the appeal they will be relieved from training, out processed per the local SOP and returned to their home state for further disposition.

k. All paperwork regarding any relief procedure will be maintained by the OCS Battalion and a copy sent to the candidates home state. Relief/disenrollment paperwork is maintained for 2 years and then destroyed IAW TR PAM 350-18 3-25 b.

l. Relief flow charts are located in the SEP (Student Evaluation Plan).

Chapter 6
LEADERSHIP RATINGS AND REPORTS

6-1. General. Each individual has the capability to lead others. The primary function of this program is to develop and assess this capability so that the individual not only has the capability, but the ability to lead others. In accomplishing this, the personnel upon whom this responsibility has been placed use many tools; pressure, encouragement, explanation, reprimands, counseling, etc. The cadre and staff are here to develop leaders who can assume the responsibilities and duties of commissioned officers. The goal is that by the completion of the course of instruction, every Officer Candidate will possess the necessary qualities of leadership. Leadership development of the Officer Candidate is **progressive** throughout the course and is accomplished through practical application (leadership positions, assignments, additional duties, etc), developmental counseling and other appropriate instructional media.

   a. This chapter provides the necessary guidance for employing the Leadership Assessment Program (LAP).

   (1) The primary purpose of OCS is to develop and assess leadership. Therefore, the primary focus of an evaluation must be directed to assessing candidate performance in this area. While total objectivity can never be obtained, the use of standardized forms and definitions will greatly enhance impartial leadership evaluation.

   (2) The OCS Leadership Assessment Program is implemented in a physically and mentally demanding environment. Its foundation is in FM 6-22, chapters 2, 4, 5 and 6. The candidate is evaluated on the Army Values, required actions, skills and attributes as defined and described in FM 6-22.

   (3) The standard established in the LAP is the leadership performance expected of a *Second Lieutenant*. Candidates are evaluated on their ability to meet this established standard. Those who possess the actions, skills and attributes necessary to become successful leaders will be commissioned as Second Lieutenants.

   (4) The leadership evaluation of candidates has two principal parts: evaluations performed by Platoon Trainers and peer evaluations/ratings performed by OC's. The greatest weight is given to the Platoon Trainer assessments. It is the Platoon Trainer who is expected to know what is expected of a Second Lieutenant.

6-2. Evaluation Tools.

   a. Leadership evaluation in OCS measures observed performance, not potential. OCS is structured to afford each candidate ample opportunity to perform and demonstrate their leadership capabilities while functioning as a member of the candidate chain of command. Candidates take on the various roles of leadership typically found in an Infantry company: commander, executive officer, first sergeant, platoon leader, platoon sergeant, and squad leader. While in these positions, candidates are expected to demonstrate the appropriate level of command presence and accomplish the duties and responsibilities of that role.

   b. The OCS Leadership Assessment Program uses six forms that are used to record observations and form the basis for counseling:

   (1) <u>Leadership Evaluation In-Brief</u>, ARNGOCS Form 2.

   (2) <u>Candidate Self-Assessment Report</u>, ARNGOCS Form 4.

   (3) <u>Leadership Observation Report</u>, ARNGOCS Form 3.

   (4) <u>Leadership Evaluation Report</u>, ARNGOCS Form 1.

   (5) Field Leadership Evaluation Report, ARNGOCS Form 5. Used only during short duration field evaluations such as evaluations of the tactical exercise without troops, and squad operations or platoon operations associated with FLX II.

   (6) Leadership Reaction Course Report (LRCR) ARNGOCS Form 7. Used on evaluations for the leadership reaction course (LRC).

Officer Candidate Guide   May 2011

c. Definitions of ratings: Candidates are evaluated on the LER and FLER using a E-S-N scale. This scale and the formal evaluation process are used to introduce the process of formal evaluation to the officer candidate. This process readies the OCs for the officer evaluation reports that they receive as second lieutenants.

(1) The candidate receives an '**E**' if she/he did an **excellent** job, consistently exceeded the standard of a BOLC A candidate, and demonstrated values, actions, skills and attributes of a newly commissioned second lieutenant. The candidate demonstrated the ability to operate independently outside of the company and battalion with limited guidance and supervision.

(2) The candidate receives an '**S**' if she/he was **satisfactory** at demonstrating the values, actions, skills and attributes expected of an officer candidate. The candidate demonstrated the minimum standard.

(3) The candidate receives an '**N**' if she/he demonstrated a **not satisfactory** performance, failed to meet the standard and did not demonstrate the values, actions skills and attributes expected of an officer candidate.

CANDIDATE SELF-ASSESSMENT REPORT				
CANDIDATE	CO / PLT	DUTY POSITION	DURATION	DATE
Birchfield, William J	A 2nd	PLT Leader	Feb IDT	02FEB06

SUMMARY OF PERFORMANCE (Give the Time, the Event, and the Result)

Time: 1105

Event: Formation to move to chow. I turned the platoon over to the platoon sergeant.

Result: The platoon sergeant took charge and took the platoon to chow.

Time: 1120

Event: Formation outside of dining facility. I was not in the proper position. CPT Ray asked me if I was 6 steps in front of the platoon.

Result: I corrected my position in the formation.

REFERENCE OC GUIDE

Candidate Self Assessment Report

d. The LER or FLER assessment is purposely subjective. It relies on the platoon trainers professional assessment. This subjectivity allows the platoon trainer to weight certain areas over others based on their experience and professional opinion of the observed behaviors. It is important to keep in mind that the candidates demonstrated leadership performance is evaluated against the standard of a second lieutenant and not in comparison to his/her peers.

e. A candidates LER or FLER scores are placed on the End of Course Summary. All LAP forms are then filed in the individual training record IAW Chapter 4, paragraph 4-2 of the OCS CMP. These forms provide the documentation required to support confirmation of honors to the candidate, or to recommend the candidate for relief from OCS, or recycle. It is imperative that careful consideration and vigilance is taken when completing and maintaining all LAP forms.

6-3. Leadership Counseling. Candidates must be counseled on their performance at the completion of every leadership position assignment. The LER counseling session occurs within 24 duty hours of the completion of the leadership assignment in all phases. FLER counseling should occur within 6 hours of the completion of the leadership assignment when the FLER is used.

a. Initial counseling will be done within 72 hours of the start of Phase I, to include the expectations of the officer candidate, the Honor Code, review of the SEP, and review of academic and non-academic events. At the end of Phase II, an end of phase counseling will be done addressing the OCs progress, to include leadership, academics, peer evaluation ratings and physical fitness. See DA Form 4856 in Annex F.

b. LAP Packets. An LAP Packet for a leadership position for a LER will include:

(1) Leadership Evaluation In-Brief.

(2) At minimum 3 Leadership Observation Reports.

(3) Candidate Self-Assessment.

(4) Leadership Evaluation Report.

6-4. Army Values. The "BE" in the BE, KNOW, DO concept of leadership. Values are the filter for all actions, skills and attributes.

    a. Loyalty. Bear true faith and allegiance to the US Constitution, the Army, your unit and other soldiers.

    b. Duty. Fulfill your obligations.

    c. Respect. Treat people as they should be treated.

    d. Selfless Service. Put the welfare of the nation, the Army and subordinates before your own.

    e. Honor. Live up to all the Army values.

    f. Integrity. Do what is right, legally and morally.

    g. Personal Courage. Face fear, danger, or adversity (physical or moral).

6-5. Core Leader Competencies. Core Leader Competencies emphasize the roles, functions and activities of what leaders do. The following provide additional detail on component categories and actions that help convey what each competency involves.

    a. **Leads.** Leading is all about influencing others. Leaders and commanders set goals and establish a vision, and then must motivate and influence others to pursue the goals.

    (1) Leads others. Leaders motivate, inspire, and influence others to take initiative, work toward a common purpose, accomplish critical tasks, and achieve organizational objectives. Influence is focused on compelling others to go beyond their individual interests and to work for the common good.

        a. Establishes and imparts clear intent and purpose.

        b. Uses appropriate influence techniques to energize others.

        c. Conveys the significance of the work.

        d. Maintains and enforces high professional standards.

        e. Balances requirements of mission with welfare of followers.

        f. Creates and promulgates vision of the future.

    (2) Extends influence beyond the chain of command. Leaders need to influence beyond their direct lines of authority and beyond chains of command. This influence may extend to joint, interagency, intergovernmental, multinational, and other groups. In these situations, leaders use indirect means of influence: diplomacy, negotiation, mediation, arbitration, partnering, conflict, resolution, consensus building, and coordination.

        a. Understands sphere of influence, means of influence, and limits of influence.

        b. Builds trust.

        c. Negotiates for understanding, builds consensus, and resolves conflict.

        d. Builds and maintains alliances.

    (3) Leads by example. Leaders constantly serve as role models for others. Leaders will always be viewed as the example, so they must maintain standards and provide examples of effectiveness through all their actions. All Army leaders should model the Army Values. Modeling provides tangible evidence of desired behaviors and reinforces verbal guidance through demonstration of commitment and action.

        a. Displays character by modeling the Army Values consistently through actions, attitude, and communications.

        b. Exemplifies the Warrior Ethos.

c. Demonstrates commitment to the Nation, Army, unit, Soldiers, community, and multinational partners.

d. Leads with confidence in adverse situations.

e. Demonstrates technical and tactical knowledge and skills.

f. Understands the importance of conceptual skills and models them to others.

e. Seeks and is open to diverse ideas and points of view.

(4) Communicates. Leaders communicate effectively by clearly expressing ideas and actively listening to others. By understanding the nature and importance of communication and practicing effective communication techniques, leaders will relate better to others and be able to translate goals into actions. Communication is essential to all other leadership competencies.

a. Listens actively.

b. Determines information-sharing strategies.

c. Employs engaging communication techniques.

d. Conveys thoughts and ideas to ensure shared understanding.

e. Presents recommendations so others understand advantages.

f. Is sensitive to cultural factors in communication.

b. Develops. Developing the organization, the second category, involves three competencies: creating a positive environment in which the organization can flourish, preparing oneself, and developing other leaders.

(1) Creates a positive environment. Leaders have the responsibility to establish and maintain positive expectations and attitudes that produce the setting for healthy relationships and effective work behaviors. Leaders are charged with improving the organization while accomplishing missions. They should leave the organization better than it was when they arrived.

a. Fosters teamwork, cohesion, cooperation, and loyalty.

b. Encourages subordinates to exercise initiative, accept responsibility, and take ownership.

c. Creates a learning environment.

d. Encourages open and candid communications.

e. Encourages fairness and inclusiveness.

f. Expresses and demonstrates care for people and their well-being.

g. Anticipates people's on-the-job needs.

h. Sets and maintains high expectations for individuals and teams.

i. Accepts reasonable setbacks and failures.

(2) Prepares Self. Leaders ensure they are prepared to execute their leadership responsibilities fully. They are aware of their limitations and strengths and seek to develop themselves. Leaders maintain physical fitness and mental well-being. They continue to improve the domain knowledge required of their leadership roles and their profession. Only through continuous preparation for missions and other challenges, being aware of self and situations and practicing lifelong learning and development can an individual fulfill the responsibilities of leadership.

a. Maintains mental and physical health and well-being.

b. Maintains self awareness: employs self understanding, and recognizes impact on others.

c. Evaluates and incorporates feedback from others.

d. Expands knowledge of technical, technological, and tactical areas.

e. Expands conceptual and interpersonal capabilities.

f. Analyzes and organizes information to create knowledge.

g. Maintains relevant cultural awareness.

h. Maintains relevant geopolitical awareness.

(3) Develop Others. Leaders encourage and support others to grow as individuals and teams. They facilitate the achievement of organizational goals through assisting others to develop. They prepare others to assume new positions elsewhere in the organization, making the organization more versatile and productive.

a. Assesses current developmental needs of others.

b. Fosters job development, job challenge, and job enrichment

c. Counsels, coaches, and mentors.

d. Facilitates ongoing development.

e. Supports institutional-based development.

f. Builds team or group skills and processes.

c. Achieves. Achieving is the third competency goal. Ultimately, leaders exist to accomplish those endeavors that the Army has prescribed for them. Getting results, accomplishing the mission, and fulfilling goals and objectives are all ways to say that leaders exist at the discretion of the organization to achieve something of value.

(1) Gets Results. A leader's ultimate purpose is to accomplish organizational results. A leader gets results by providing guidance and managing resources, as well as performing the other leader competencies. This competency is focused on consistent and ethical task accomplishment through supervising, managing, monitoring and controlling of the work.

a. Prioritizes, organizes, and coordinates tasking for teams or other organizational structures/groups.

b. Identifies and accounts for individual and group capabilities and commitment to task.

c. Designates, clarifies, and de-conflicts roles.

d. Identifies, contends for, allocates, and manages resources.

e. Removes work barriers.

f. Recognizes and rewards good performance.

g. Seeks, recognizes, and takes advantage of opportunities to improve performance.

h. Makes feedback part of work processes.

i. Executes plans to accomplish the mission.

j. Identifies and adjusts to external influences on the mission or tasking and organization

6-6. Leadership Attributes. The core leader competencies are complemented by attributes that distinguish high performing leaders of character. Attributes are characteristics that are an inherent part of an individual's total core, physical, and intellectual aspects. Attributes shape how an individual behaves in their environment. Attributes for Army leaders are aligned to identity, presence, and intellectual capacity.

(1) A Leader of Character (Identity). Factors internal and central to a leader, that which makes up an individual's core.

a. Army Values.

b. Empathy.

c. Warrior Ethos.

(2) A Leader with Presence. How a leader is perceived by others based on the leader's outward appearance, demeanor, actions, and words.

a. Military Bearing.

b. Physically Fit.

c. Confident.

d. Resilient.

(3) A Leader with Intellectual Capacity. The mental resources or tendencies that shape a leader's conceptual abilities and impact of effectiveness.

a. Agility.

b. Judgment.

c. Innovative.

d. Interpersonal tact.

e. Domain Knowledge.

6-7. Leadership Positions.

a. Student Leadership Tour of Duty. The Senior Platoon Trainer will establish and assign the student chain-of-command and ensure **each OC is rated a minimum of one time during the each phase.** Tours of duty last for 24 hours during phase I and can be longer in phase II and III.

b. **Prior to each tour of duty** a Candidate In-brief form & counseling by the Platoon Trainer will be completed.

c. **Upon completion of each tour of duty** in the student chain-of-command, the OC will:

(1) Complete a Candidate Self-Assessment Report. This will be turned into the Platoon Trainer within the prescribed time. Utilize the TER (Time, Event, Result) format for completion.

(2) Will receive a completed Leadership Evaluation Report (LER) counseling by the Platoon Trainer. This will occur in conjunction with a formal counseling. **This must be completed within 24 hours.**

(3) Thoroughly brief the incoming chain-of-command. This briefing will include all of the necessary information required for the new chain-of-command to carry on with the mission and conduct follow-on business.

d. Duties and Responsibilities. The chain-of-command determines how to efficiently use their time, manpower, and materials to accomplish assigned tasks. Rated positions within the Company chain-of-command are:

(1) Candidate Company Commander (CO)

(2) Candidate Executive Officer (XO)

(3) Candidate First Sergeant (1SG)

(4) Candidate Platoon Leader (PL)

(5) Candidate Platoon Sergeant (PSG)

(6) Candidate Squad Leader (SL)

6-8. Leadership Evaluations.

a. Leadership evaluations are conducted by Platoon Trainers.

b. Leadership Evaluation Report (LER): The LER rates the OC on Army Values, actions, skills and attributes using a E – S – N rating scale. The Platoon Trainer must rate as many areas as possible depending on their observations made during the tour of duty.

c. Field Leadership Evaluation Report (FLER): The FLER rates the OC of the 8 steps of the troop leading process during field training. The FLER uses the E – S – N rating scale. All of the troop leading procedures will be evaluated.

d. Leadership Observation Report (LOR): The LOR records a single action of the OC. The OC does not have to be in a leadership position to receive a LOR. It is used as an observation tool and not an assessment in and of itself; however, a series of LORs in an OC's file over time will reveal trends-positive or negative-of that OC's performance and abilities. LORs are taken into account when LERs are used to rate the Candidate Chain of Command. Utilize the TER format for the completion of the LOR.

e. DA Form 4856 Counseling Statement: The DA Form 4856 will be used to counsel an OC for outstanding positive or negative academic, leadership, or other actions and behavior. Also used for initial, mid-cycle, close out or end-of-phase counseling, peer evaluation results, prerequisite or missing item counseling, academic or performance deficiencies, and any time it's deemed appropriate to document behavior or a situation. The DA 4856 will be completed by a Platoon Trainer officer or NCO or appropriate individuals in the chain of command as necessary.

f. Instructors: Instructors may utilize the DA Form 4856 or the Leadership Observation Report when they see remarkable examples of strong or weak leadership.

g. Officer Candidates:

(1). Candidate Self-Assessment Report: The candidate self-assessment report is completed by the OC during and following a tour of duty in a leadership position. This report provides information concerning the OC's perception of their performance. Utilize the TER format for the completion of the Self-Assessment Report.

(2) Candidates Plan for Improvement: The candidate will fill out their Plan for Improvement located on the back of the LER, after they have been counseled by the Platoon Trainer Officer/NCO

(3) Peer Evaluations

(a) A part of the OCS Program involves teaching the candidate how to assess leadership performance in his peers and subordinates. The peer rating process is used as a vehicle to these ends.

(b). Cadre members are not able to evaluate many of the intrinsic dynamics of the squad. Peer evaluations disclose to the OCS Cadre the "silent" leadership characteristics of a class. It can also be useful to discover how each candidate perceives their own progress in the course in relation to his peers.

(c) The peer evaluations help the candidate focus on patterns of behavior they would not otherwise see. This process provides them with insight into how others perceive their leadership style and attitude.

(d) Additionally, OCs must be prepared to objectively evaluate subordinates upon commissioning. Each OC will rank their fellow squad members numerically from first to last. The OC will also provide a brief but concise statement as to the leadership strengths and weaknesses that prompted them to place their fellow OCs in these positions. This statement must comment on performance in the leadership traits, which resulted in the rating.

Officer Candidate Guide   May 2011

Chapter 7

ORGANIZATION OF CANDIDATE COMPANIES

7-1. General.

a. Officer Candidates occupy all of the command and leadership positions within the OCS companies. A normal tour of duty is 24 hours in length; however, tours of duty during Phase II and Phase III are situational dependant and are at the discretion of the Platoon Trainer Staff.

b. Company organization:

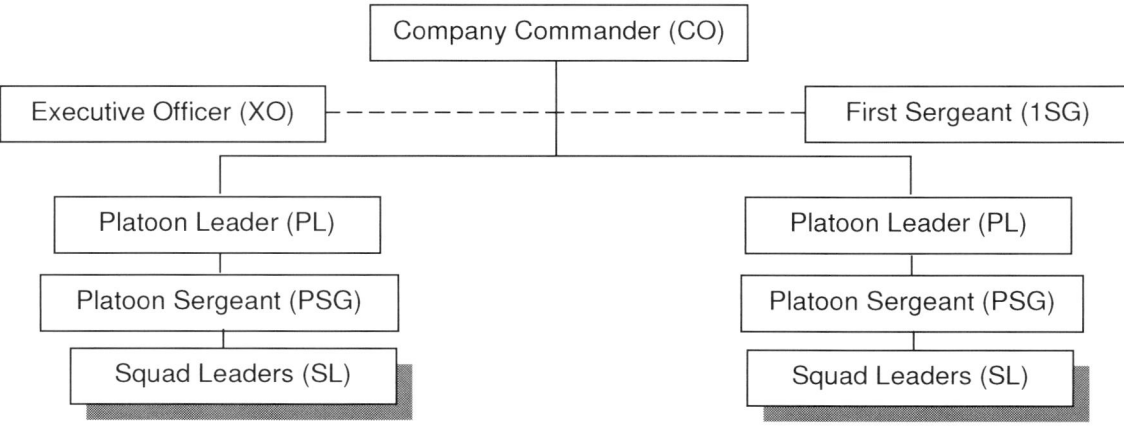

7-2. Duties of the Chain of Command.

a. Company Commander (CO).

(1) General Duties: The Candidate Company Commander is responsible for all that the Company does or fails to do. He plans, makes timely decisions, issues orders, delegates tasks, and personally supervises Company activities. The primary responsibility of the student commander is to gain and maintain control of the company, set the example for his company.

(2). The Candidate Commander exercises command through the Candidate Executive Officer (XO), Candidate First Sergeant (1SG), and Candidate Platoon Leaders (PL's).

(3) He is responsible for the morale, welfare, control, and discipline of the Company. He will:

   a. Supervise the XO and 1SG in accomplishing their missions.

   b. Supervise PL's in supporting and enforcing all standards, policies, and procedures set forth in the OCS program. Take positive action to correct deficiencies.

   c. Be responsible for all status reports.

   d. Move the Company to and from instruction areas in a military manner.

   e. Enforce all policies and procedures for proper conduct of course.

   f. The CO must know his duties, responsibilities and actions IAW FM 3-21.5 (D&C).

   g. When training at platoon level the CO will attend all training periods with his platoon.

   h. In the absence of specific instructions, guidance or orders, the CO will make those decisions necessary to accomplish the mission in accordance with established procedures, safety considerations and common sense.

b. Executive Officer (XO).

Officer Candidate Guide   May 2011

(1) General Duties; The XO is the principal assistant to the Candidate Commander. The XO should do everything possible to relieve the Commander of administrative burdens through the proper management of his resources.

(2) The XO acts as the chief advisor to the Commander and assumes command to the Company in the absence of the commander.

(3) The XO coordinates with the principal instructor for each block of instruction before scheduled training for any special requirements. Upon receiving those instructions, he will report to the CO.

(4) The XO coordinates with the Platoon Trainer Company Commander and Food Service Manager for special and ordinary mess needs, including special rations, changes in mess times, and amendments to and implementation of Dining Facility policies.

(5) The XO coordinates with the Platoon Trainer Company Commander and Platoon Trainer Company Executive Officer for arms issue and turn-in. The XO supervises all supply operations and arrangements.

(6) The XO monitors heat categories and other natural dangers, which threaten warm-weather training, and reports any dangers up the chain-of-command immediately.

(7) The XO must know his duties, responsibilities and actions IAW FM 3-21.5 (D&C).

(8) The XO is responsible for barracks and building security to include the location of all keys.

(9) The XO is responsible for all sensitive items.

(10) The XO will ensure that all Officer Candidates report for formal counseling (Performance Counseling) with a Self-Assessment Report (SAR).

(11) The XO maintains the XO's book and has it ready for inspection at all times. The XO's book will be neat, presentable, and updated. At a minimum, it includes the following.

a. Medical Evacuation Procedures

b. Emergency First-Aid Procedures

c. Training Schedule

d. DFAC Menu and Schedule

e. Daily Weather Information, with Wet Bulb Information, if applicable

f. Current OC Roster

g. Platoon Trainer Duty Roster to include building numbers, room numbers and phone numbers

h. Installation Maps (Cantonment and Tactical)

i. Relevant Installation telephone and building numbers

j. Tabbed FM 3-21.5 (Drill and Ceremony)

k. Tabbed TC 3-22.20 (Physical Readiness Training)

l. AR 670-1 (Wear and Appearance of Army Uniforms and Insignia)

m. AR 25-50 (Preparing and Managing Correspondence)

c. First Sergeant (1SG).

(1) General Duties: The 1SG monitors and coordinates control of all matters pertaining to logistical requirements and administrative actions. Active communication and supervision through the Platoon Sergeants is essential; however, this communication will complement the formal chain-of-command not circumvent it.

(2) Accountability: Accountability of all soldiers is an essential and constant process of updates. The 1SG will maintain an accurate accountability status report at all times. (This will be defaulted to the PSG when platoon level training is incurred.) The 1SG will prepare a report of the Company accountability and submit it to the Company Platoon Trainer or his representative. This report will be updated following formations or changes in personnel status. This report should be generated prior to formation whenever possible to provide for time

constraints. PSGs will make an informal report to include any OCs not present for duty and the reason for their absence. The completed report will include:

    a. Number of OCs Assigned

    b. Number of OCs Present

    c. Names of absent OCs

    d. Reason OC is absent

    e. Estimated time of Return for Absent OCs

(3) The 1SG will form the company and receive report IAW FM 3-21.5, Chapter 7.

(4) The 1SG must set the example for all NCOs.

(5) The 1SG must know his duties, responsibilities and actions IAW FM 3-21.5 (D&C).

(6) The 1SG must monitor and coordinate all mess, logistics and company administration needs with the XO.

(7) When training is conducted at platoon level, the 1SG will train with his platoon.

(8) The 1SG will ensure at least one police call is conducted of his company area during his tour of duty.

  d. Platoon Leader (PL).

(1) General Duties: The PL commands the platoon and is responsible for the morale, welfare, and discipline of his subordinates. The Platoon Leader is ultimately responsible for everything the platoon does or fails to do.

(2) The PL commands primarily through Squad Leaders (SL), delegating authority through the Platoon Sergeant.

(3) The PL must set the example for his platoon.

(4) The PL must know his duties, responsibilities and actions IAW FM 3-21.5 (D&C).

(5) The Platoon Leader will ensure that:

    a. Proper accountability is maintained.

    b. PSG and SLs fulfill their responsibilities.

    c. Platoon members receive necessary information for the platoon to accomplish assigned missions.

    d. An equitable distribution of details and privileges exists and OC's personal needs are taken care of.

    e. SLs inspect their squads before each formation and correct deficiencies.

    f. OCs are spot-checked for appearance, required knowledge, and preparedness for training.

    g. Platoon, Platoon Trainer Officers receive daily briefings of the status of the platoon. This briefing includes, but is not limited to, morale, personnel problems, inspection results, anticipated problems, and planned courses of action for improving platoon performance.

    h. OCs inspect weapons, maintain accountability of all sensitive items, and platoon equipment before and during training, and before turn-in.

    i. A Platoon notebook is maintained with an annotated platoon roster, broken down by squad.

  e. Platoon Sergeant (PSG).

(1) General Duties: The PSG is the principle assistant to the platoon leader and will assume command of the platoon in the absence of the platoon leader.

(2) The PSG must know his duties, responsibilities and actions IAW FM 3-21.5 (D&C).

(3) The PSG monitors and coordinates all logistical and administrative needs with the 1SG.

(4) The PSG will:

a. Maintain accurate accountability of platoon members, accountability of sensitive items and platoon equipment at all times and keep the chain-of-command informed of the accountability status.

b. Conduct formations in accordance with FM 3-21.5 and the OC Guide.

c. Enforce the regulations and directives of OCS.

d. Ensure the platoon maintains and accounts for assigned equipment at all times.

e. Relay pertinent information to the platoon in a timely manner.

f. Maintain control of and ensure compliance of all SOPs.

g. Assist the PL in conducting inspections.

h. Ensure the platoon bulletin board is up to date.

f. Squad Leader (SL).

(1) General Duties: The SL is the direct supervisor of the individual squad members.

(2) The SL must know his duties, responsibilities and actions IAW FM 3-21.5 (D&C).

(3) The SL will ensure that:

a. Squad status is maintained, including the location and activity of members.

b. Squad members maintain and account for all issued property.

c. Personal appearance, uniform appearance, and personal hygiene of all squad members are to the highest possible standards.

d. The squad is prepared to accomplish assigned missions.

e. The squad's billeting area is inspection-ready at all times.

f. The squad completes all details to the highest standards possible.

g. Each OC knows the mission to be accomplished and the required knowledge material.

h. All squad members are informed.

7-3 Using the Chain of Command. The Chain of Command is a tool for command and communication. Messages flow both down and up. It is a dynamic system with only one concrete concept: It must follow the company rank structure. The following is an example of its use (8 Troop Leading Procedures):

a. The CO receives a task from higher up (training schedule, Platoon Trainer Officer, etc.) (#1 Receive the Mission). The CO issues a warning order to the XO, PL's and the 1SG (#2 Issue a Warning Order). The warning order should contain Situation, Mission, a Tentative Plan, Special Equipment Requirements, Uniform, Time and Place of OPORD. While the CO prepares his OPORD (#3 Make a Tentative Plan), the PLs will issue a warning order to their PSGs and platoons. The XO will prepare to procure items necessary for the company to complete its mission (classrooms, training aids, arrange for food) (#4 Initiate Necessary Movement & #5 Reconnoiter). This will be accomplished through the S4 (supply and logistics). The 1SG will assist the XO by collecting requests from the PSGs. The PL will work with the PSG to ready the platoon for the mission. The PSG will coordinate and delegate tasks to the SLs to ready their squads for action (proper uniform and equipment, water...).

b. The CO will use all available information gathered from the XO and 1SG during the reconnaissance process for his Operation Order (#6 Complete the Plan). The XO, PLs and 1SG will meet the CO at the predetermined time and location to receive the OPORD. The CO will issue the OPORD (#7 Issue the Complete OPORD). The CO will then conduct rehearsals for the operation (#8 Supervise & Refine. **This is critical to the success or failure of the mission.**)

c. Once the OPORD is issued; the XO will make final requests and preparations. The PLs, using the CO OPORD, will write their platoon OPORDs. They will then issue their OPORDs to the PSGs and platoons. Final preparations and request will be made. The 1SG is responsible for having the company formed and accounted for at the appropriate time.

This is not the only way to use the Chain of Command. Being a dynamic system, it can be manipulated to fit any situation. Creativity with its use will be a measure of success as an OC leader.

7-4. The Five-Paragraph Operation Order. The OPORD is the CO's written plan for the mission. It contains 5 paragraphs. (Refer to FM 3-21.8 Chapter 5).

Task Organization – Explains how the unit is organized for the operation.

1. Situation – Provides information essential to the subordinate leader's understanding of the situation.

a. Enemy forces

(1) Disposition, composition and strength

(2) Capabilities

(3) Most Probable Course of Action

b. Friendly forces

(1) Higher Unit

(2) Left Unit's Mission

(3) Right Unit's Mission

(4) Forward Unit's Mission

c. Attachments and Detachments

2. Mission – Provide a clear and concise statement of the task to be accomplished and the purpose for doing it. (Who, What, When Where, and Why)

3. Execution

Intent – Give the stated vision that defines the purpose of the operation and the desired end state.

a. Concept of the Operation – Explanation, in general terms, HOW the platoon, as a whole, will accomplish the mission. Identify the most important task for the platoon. Attempt to limit this paragraph to six sentences.

(1) Maneuver – Address all squads and attachments by name, giving each of them an essential task.

(2) Fires – Refer to the concept of fire support to synchronize and complement the scheme of maneuver.

b. Tasks to Maneuver Units - Specific instructions for subordinate elements other than those in Paragraph 3.a.(1).

c. Tasks to Combat Support Units – if attached.

d. Coordinating Instructions – List the details of coordination and control applicable to two or more units in the platoon. May include timeline, MOPP Level, order of march, etc.

4. Service support – **(Sustainment)** (This paragraph is of particular interest to the XO and 1SG)

a. General – Refer to any SOP's that govern the sustainment of the operation.

b. Material & Services.

(1) Supply - List needed supplies and services.

(2) Transportation - Schedule, constraints and limitations, and methods.

(3) Services.

(4) Maintenance.

(5) Medical Evacuation.

(a) Personnel

(b) Miscellaneous

5. Command and Signal (Command and Control)
- a. Command
    - (1) Location of commanders
    - (2) Location of second in command
    - (3) Succession of command
- b. Signal
    - (1) SOI if appropriate
    - (2) Emergency signals if necessary
    - (3) Challenge / Password

Officer Candidate Guide					May 2011

Chapter 8
TRAINING

8-1. Pre-OCS Requirements.

    a. APFT # 1 – Must pass standard APFT IAW TC 3-22.20 within 60 days of (and prior to day one of) Phase I training.

    b. Course prerequisites – Must provide all required documentation to confirm candidate meets course prerequisites prior to the start of Phase I.

8-2. Phase I Requirements. The following events must be successfully completed prior to the end of Phase I.

    a. Five-mile foot march - Must complete five-mile foot march without assistance within 1 hour and 45 minutes. Uniform must include ACU, LBE/LBV, KEVLAR, M16 Rifle, and ruck sack (35-40 lbs not including water).

    b. Peer evaluation # 1 – Must complete peer evaluation # 1.

    c. POI Training – Must attend or makeup all Phase I POI training.

    d. Examinations – Must pass all four Phase I exams or retests. Candidate must score 70% or greater on each exam. Phase I exams include: Training Management, Land Navigation Written, Land Navigation Day Practical, and Land Navigation Night Practical. All exams and retest must be completed prior to the end of Phase I.

    e. Leadership Position Evaluations – Must receive and complete a minimum of one leadership position evaluation during Phase I. See Chapter 6 of this OC Guide for details concerning the Leadership Assessment Program.

    f. Warrior Task Battle Drills (WTBD) – Candidates must instruct at least one of the WTBDs and demonstrate task mastery through skill application of all WTBDs. Candidates must receive a go on all WTBDs and have documented evidence of task mastery on each task.

    g. Must be recommended by the OCS company commander (by signature on End of Course Summary Sheet Phase I) as possessing the ability to acquire the leadership skills, attitudes and knowledge required of a second lieutenant prior to graduating Phase I training and beginning Phase II training.

8-3. Phase II Requirements. The following events must be successfully completed prior to the end of Phase II.

    a. Peer evaluation # 2 - Must complete peer evaluation # 2.

    b. POI Training – Must attend or makeup all Phase II POI training.

    c. Examinations – Must pass all eight Phase II exams or retests. Candidate must score 70% or greater on each exam. Phase II exams include: Operations, Tactics, Call for Fire, Leadership, Military Justice, Heritage and History, Supply Activities and Elements of Military Intelligence. All exams and retest must be completed prior to the end of Phase II.

    d. Peer evaluation # 3 - Must complete peer evaluation # 3.

    e. Seven-mile foot march - Must complete the seven mile foot march without assistance within 2 hours and 30 minutes. Uniform must include BDU/ACU, LBE/LBV, KEVLAR, M16 Rifle, and ruck sack (must weigh between 35-40 lbs, not including water, at the beginning and completion of the foot march).

    f. Ten-mile foot march - Must complete the ten-mile foot march without assistance within 3 hours and 30 minutes. Uniform must include ACU, LBE/LBV, KEVLAR, M16 Rifle, and ruck sack (must weigh between 35-40 lbs, not including water, at the beginning and completion of the foot march).

    g. APFT # 2 - Must pass standard APFT IAW TC 3-22.20 within 60 days of Phase III start date. For Accelerated OCS Phase II APFT # 2 must be prior to and within 20 days of Phase III start date.

    h. Three Mile Release Run - Must complete a three mile release run without assistance, within the designated time standard. Standards, male 27:00 minutes (9 min per mile) and female 29 minutes and 15 seconds (9:45 per mile). One retest will be given to a candidate who fails to meet the required time standard. Uniform will be the IPFU.

i. Leadership Position Evaluations – Must receive and complete a minimum of one leadership position evaluation during Phase II. See Chapter 6 of this OC Guide for details concerning the Leadership Assessment Program.

j. Must receive an "E" or an "S" on leadership evaluation and must be recommended by the OCS company commander (by signature on End of Course Summary Sheet Phase II) as possessing the ability to acquire the leadership skills, attitudes and knowledge required of a second lieutenant prior to graduating Phase II training and beginning Phase III training.

8-4. Phase III Requirements. The following events must be successfully completed prior to the end of Phase III.

a. Combat Water Survival Test – Must attempt the 3 event combat water swim test.

b. Obstacle or Confidence Course. Must conduct obstacle or confidence course training and make a valid attempt at each obstacle on the course.

c. POI Training – Must attend all Phase III POI training.

d. Leadership Reaction Course (LRC) – Must participate as a squad member and as a squad leader at LRC training.

e. Leadership Position Evaluations – Must receive and complete a minimum of one leadership position evaluation during Phase III (LRC). This evaluation is in addition to the evaluation the candidate receives during FLX II. Candidate must attain an "E" or an "S" on their FLX II evaluation to graduate from Phase III. See Chapter 6 of this OC Guide for details concerning the Leadership Assessment Program.

f. Must be recommended by the OCS company commander (by signature on End of Course Summary Sheet Phase III) as possessing the leadership skills, attitudes and knowledge required of a second lieutenant prior to graduating Phase III and OCS

Officer Candidate Guide   May 2011

Chapter 9
REQUIRED KNOWLEDGE

9-1. Requirements. The following is the list of required knowledge. The Platoon Trainer Staff will inform the officer candidates of the suspense by which they must be able to recite each item verbatim.

  a. Chain of Command.

<u>Permanent Chain of Command</u>

Commander in Chief	State Assistant Adjutant General, Army
Secretary of Defense	RTI Commander
Secretary of the Army	Battalion Commander
Chairman, Joint Chiefs of Staff	Senior Platoon Trainer Officer
Army Chief of Staff	Company Commander
Chief, NGB	First Sergeant
State Adjutant General	Platoon, Platoon Trainer Officer/NCO

  b. OCS Honor Code.

   An Officer Candidate will not lie, cheat, or steal, nor tolerate those who do.

  c. General Orders.

   1. I will guard everything within the limits of my post and quit my post only when properly relieved.

   2. I will obey my special orders and perform all my duties in a military manner.

   3. I will report violations of my special orders, emergencies and anything not covered in my instructions to the Commander of the Relief.

  d. Army Values.

   (1) Loyalty: Bear true faith and allegiance to the U.S. Constitution, the Army, and other soldiers.

   (2) Duty: Fulfill your obligations.

   (3) Respect: Treat people as they should be treated.

   (4) Selfless-Service: Put the welfare of the nation, the Army and your subordinates before your own.

   (5) Honor: Live up to all the Army values.

   (6) Integrity: Do what's right, legally and morally.

   (7) Personal Courage: Face fear, danger, or adversity (physical and moral).

  e. LEADERSHIP DEFINED (FM 6-22). Leadership is influencing people-by providing purpose, direction and motivation-while operating to accomplish the mission and improving the organization

  f. The Troop Leading Procedures.

   (1) Receive the Mission

   (2) Issue the Warning Order

   (3) Make a Tentative Plan

   (4) Initiate Necessary Troop Movement

   (5) Conduct Reconnaissance

   (6) Complete the Plan

   (7) Issue the Complete Order

   (8) Supervise

g. The Estimate of the Situation.

  (1) Detailed mission analysis.

  (2) Situation and courses of action.

  (3) Analyze courses of action; wargame.

  (4) Compare courses of action.

  (5) Decision.

h. The Five-Paragraph Operation Order.

  TASK ORGANIZATION

  (1) SITUATION

  (2) MISSION

  (3) EXECUTION

  (4) SERVICE SUPPORT   (SUSTAINMENT)

  (5) COMMAND AND SIGNAL (COMMAND AND CONTROL)

i. SALUTE REPORT:

  S - Size

  A - Activity

  L - Location

  U - Uniform

  T - Time

  E - Equipment

j. Code of Conduct.

I am an American fighting man. I serve in the forces which guard my country and our way of life. I am prepared to give my life in their defense.

I will never surrender of my own free will. If in command I will never surrender my men while they still have the means to resist.

If I am captured I will continue to resist by all means available. I will make every effort to escape and will aid others to escape. I will accept neither parole nor special favors from the enemy.

If I become a prisoner of war, I will keep faith with my fellow prisoners. I will give no information or take part in any action which might be harmful to my comrades. If I am senior, I will take command. If not, I will obey the lawful orders of those appointed over me and will back them up in every way.

When questioned, should I become a prisoner of war, I am required to give only my name, rank, service number, and date of birth. I will evade further questions to the best of my ability. I will make no oral or written statements disloyal to my country and its allies or harmful to their cause.

I will never forget that I am an American fighting man, responsible for my actions, and dedicated to the principles which made my country free. I will trust in my God and in the United States of America.

k. Three Transmissions of a Call for Fire.

  (1) First transmission: Observer identification and warning order.

    Example: H24 THIS IS N59, ADJUST FIRE, OVER

  (2) Second transmission: Target location.

    Example: GRID CF123456, OVER

(3) Third transmission: Target description, method of engagement method of fire and control.

Example: TANK IN OPEN, ICM IN EFFECT, OVER

l. 9-Line Medevac Request.

    Line 1: Location of pickup site.

    Line 2: Frequency and call sign at pickup site.

    Line 3: Number of patients by precedence (Urgent, Priority, Routine, Convenience).

    Line 4: Special equipment required.

    Line 5: Number of patients by type (# litter & # ambulatory).

    Line 6: Type of wound, injury, illness.

    Line 7: Method of marking pickup site.

    Line 8: Patient nationality and status.

    Line 9: Landing Zone description.

m. Terrain Analysis (OACOK)

    Obstacles

    Avenues of Approach

    Cover and Concealment

    Observation and Fields of Fire

    Key Terrain

n. METT-TC

    Mission

    Enemy

    Troops

    Terrain

    Time Available

    Civilian Considerations

APPENDIX A
PACKING LIST

INSERT LOCAL PACKING LIST

Officer Candidate Guide   May 2011

APPENDIX B

CANDIDATE AUTOBIOGRAPHY

PREPARING THE OCS STUDENT AUTOBIOGRAPHY

B-1. SUBJECT AREA: Written Communication.

B-2. ASSIGNMENT: Write an OCS Student autobiography of 4-5 pages (1000 words max.)

B-3. ASSIGNMENT INFORMATION:

a. Substance: Generally speaking, a writer reflects upon and describes his/her life, or part of it, in an autobiography. For your first assignment as an OCS student, we ask that you write an OCS Student autobiography, focusing on that part of your life which has led you to consider becoming an Army Officer. Here are some suggestions for proceeding with this assignment:

(1) Present vital statistics: date, place of birth, places of residence, schools you have attended, family background, and prior military service or experiences.

(2) Describe special events in your life; relate circumstances and happenings that make you different, that help make you what you are, and that you expect your audience to find memorable.

(3) Tell what you expect to contribute to society through gaining an education and what you may contribute by completing OCS requirements and gaining a commission.

NOTE: One of your principle writing tasks is to develop a fluid, readable narrative of your life, so do not merely list responses to these suggested questions. Instead, weave your responses into a narrative story of your life and your expectations in life and how this relates to your goal of earning a commission in the military.

b. Format: Final paper will be typed or computer-printed on one side only. Number each page (except the first page-cover sheet) on the center bottom of the page. The cover sheet format is provided. Your autobiography will start on the second page and be numbered "1" in the numbering sequence of all the remaining pages.

c. Fasten a head and shoulders photo of yourself (3" x 5" or 4" x 6" photos or digital camera printouts on high-quality paper are acceptable) in uniform ACUs) to the bottom of the cover sheet. Use "Scotch Magic Tape" to fasten photo to cover sheet. Local policy/SOP may require your class to schedule a date for all of you to take photos together, or you may wish to get together with classmates and take each other's picture.

d. Evaluation: OCS Staff members will evaluate your autobiography. The OCS Selection Board of Officers will read and review your autobiography to formulate initial opinions about you. Your autobiography will be judged on four criteria: content, organization, readability, and presentation. Evaluators will consider the following questions as they make their evaluation:

(1) Substance. How much specific detail have you used? (Generally, the more detail the better) How appropriate is the detail? How well does the reader get to "know" you, solely on the bases of your autobiography?

(2) Organization. Does your paper develop smoothly? Does each part relate well with the rest of your paper? Do you relate your earlier life to your present situation in college? Do your expectations regarding the future emerge clearly from what you reveal of your past and present?

(3) Style. Have you used effective transitions? Have you written directly? Have you chosen familiar, unpretentious vocabulary? Have you avoided long, cumbersome sentences? On the other hand, have you also avoided an extended series of very simply structured sentences? Has your punctuation assisted rather than hindered or confused your reader? Overall, have you observed the conventions of standard written English?

(4) Correctness. Is your text carefully proofread, and free of typographical errors? Have used the proper format? Is your text neat, and free of smudges and wrinkles?

OCS Student Autobiography

By

NAME: (Last, First, Middle)

OCS Program (State)

OCS Class Number

Date Prepared

Candidate Photo

CLOTHING & EQUIPMENT DISPLAYS

INSERT

LOCAL DISPLAYS

Officer Candidate Guide

May 2011

APPENDIX D
CONTRABAND

D-1. Contraband. The following items are considered contraband and will be secured IAW local SOP. The Platoon Trainer staff may grant use of some of these items during Intermediate or Senior Phase as phase privileges.

1. Tobacco products.
2. Alcohol.
3. Any supplements taken to enhance performance.
4. Medications not prescribed by a Physician.
5. Cellular Phones
6. Pagers
7. Food (to include gum, candy, cough drops, mints, etc.) No food will be taken out of the DFAC or brought back from the field.
8. Contact lenses.
9. Irons.
10. Stoves.
11. Heat tabs.
12. Cosmetics.
13. Hair nets & curlers.
14. Perfumes, colognes, or after-shave.
15. Body sprays.
16. Electric or battery operated razors.
17. Digital/tape recorders, CD players, Walkman, MP3 players, Ipods.
18. Radios, portable TV/ DVD players.
19. Laptop/Ipads/palm pilots.
20. Global positioning devices.
21. Civilian clothes.
22. Magazines and Newspapers.
23. Bayonets, fixed-blade knives, or knives over 3".
24. Any lotion other than non-scented.
25. Any handheld electronic devices (i.e., video game players, organizers).
26. Adult material of any kind.
27. Vitamins.

a. Regarding items 1-4: These items could cause severe physical harm if they are used under the strenuous conditions placed on the candidate throughout the course.

b. This list is not all-inclusive. Items that are not listed above are subject to cadre discretion. If you have questions concerning a particular item ask your Platoon, Platoon Trainer for additional guidance.

c. You will be verbally counseled on retaining any of these items. If any contraband is found on you or in your room at any time during the course you will be subject to disciplinary action.

APPENDIX E
SENIOR STATUS

E-1. General.

    a. In order for a candidate to complete the OCS program he/she must obtain Senior Status. The following are factors that are considered in order to promote a candidate to Senior Status: Leadership Evaluations, Academic Average, APFT score, and Peer Evaluations.

    b. While the OCS environment encourages teamwork and team building, Senior Status is an individual and not a collective achievement and will therefore be awarded on an individual basis. The determination of when Officer Candidates are eligible for Senior Status is at the discretion of the Senior Platoon Trainer Officer.

    c. Senior Officer Candidates are expected to uphold the highest standards. While granted more privileges, Senior Officer Candidates are expected to maintain the high level of discipline that the OCS program demands.

    d. Senior Status is not permanent. Senior Status can be removed by recommendation of the Platoon Trainer Officers and Platoon Trainer NCOs.

E-2. Senior Officer Candidate Uniform.

INSERT LOCAL SENIOR CANIDATE UNIFORM SOP

E-3. Senior Officer Candidate Privileges.

INSERT LOCAL SENIOR CANIDATE UNIFORM SOP

APPENDIX F

SAFETY AND COMPOSITE RISK MANAGEMENT

F-1. Purpose. Composite risk management (CRM) is the Army's primary decision-making process for identifying hazards and controlling risks across the full spectrum of Army missions, functions, operations, and activities.

   a. The goal of risk management is to mitigate risks associated with all hazards that have the potential to injure or kill personnel, damage or destroy equipment, or otherwise impact mission effectiveness.

   b. Army Policy on risk management. FM 5-19, Composite Risk Management (August 2006) directs leaders at all levels to effectively integrate into all Army plans, programs, decision processes, operations and activities the following principles.

      (1) Integrate Composite Risk Management into all phases of missions and operations.

      (2) Make risk decisions at the appropriate level.

      (3) Accept no unnecessary risk.

      (4) Apply the process cyclically and continuously.

      (5) Do not be risk adverse.

   c. Risk management is a systematic 5 step decision-making process by which leaders at all levels make military operations safer and more effective. The process is used to balance the mission needs against the potential losses. The goal of any leader is not to put training first or safety first, but to train safely. The key terms used in the risk management process are listed below.

      (1) Hazard. A condition with the potential to cause injury, illness, or death of personnel; damage to or loss of equipment or property; or mission degradation.

      (2) Risk. Probability and severity of loss linked to hazards.

      (3) Controls. Actions taken to eliminate hazards or to reduce their risk

      (4) Risk Assessment. The identification and assessment of hazards (the first two steps of the CRM process).

      (5) Risk Management. The process of identifying, assessing, and controlling risks arising from operational factors and making decisions that balance risk cost with mission benefits.

F-2. The Three Tiers of Safety.

   a. Tier 1 – Command Level

      (1) Provide a command climate that ties safety into force protection.

      (2) Plan and resource for safety.

      (3) Establish safety standards.

      (4) Keep training consistent with abilities.

      (5) Make risk acceptance decisions.

   b. Tier 2 – Leader Level

      (1) Reinforce command climate on safety.

      (2) Identify and eliminate or control safety hazards.

      (3) Train/emphasize/enforce performance to standard.

      (4) Assess hazards/risks.

(5) Make risk decisions; supervise and follow-up.

c. Tier 3 – Individual Level

(1) Take personal responsibility for safety/risk management.

(2) Take immediate action for unsafe acts.

(3) Modify your own risk behavior.

(4) Perform to standards.

(5) Be part of the "buddy" system.F-3.

F-3. The Risk Management Process.

a. Identify the hazards. Leaders identify potential sources of hazard or risk soldiers could encounter. The factors of mission, enemy, terrain and weather, troops and support available, time available, and civil considerations (METT-TC) serve as a standard format for identification of hazards.

b. Assess the hazards. Leaders assess hazards and risk is assigned in terms of probability and severity of adverse impact of an event/occurrence. The end result of this assessment is an initial estimate of risk for each indentified hazard expressed in terms of extremely high, high, moderate, or low as determined from the standardized risk assessment matrix.

c. Develop controls and make risk decisions.

(1) Develop Controls. Leaders develop one or more controls that either eliminate the hazard or reduce the risk of a hazardous incident occurring. Controls generally fall into three basic categories: educational, physical, or avoidance/elimination. To be effective they must by suitable, feasible, and acceptable.

(2) Reassess risk. With controls applied, risk must be reassessed to determine the residual risk associated with each hazard and the overall residual risk for the mission.

(3) Make risk decision. Leaders balance the risk or potential loss against expectations or expected gains.

d. Implement controls. Leaders ensure that controls are integrated into SOPs, written and verbal orders, mission briefings, and staff estimates.

e. Supervise and evaluate.

(1) Supervise. Supervision provides commanders and leaders with the situational awareness necessary to anticipate, identify, and assess any new hazards and to develop or modify controls as necessary.

(2) Evaluate. The evaluation process occurs during all phases of the operation, and as part of the AAR and assessment following completion of the operation or activity. Evaluation process identifies any new hazards; assesses effectiveness in supporting objectives; assesses the implementation, execution, and communication of the controls; accuracy of residual risk; and ensures compliance with the guiding principles of CRM.

F-4. Forms. The DA Form 7566, Composite Risk Management Worksheet (APR2005) will be used by candidates for the analysis of training events and to identify and reduce or implement risk mitigating measures. All candidate developed risk assessments will be approved by the TAC Staff prior to every training event. Risk Management Worksheets will be completed daily during leadership tours, additional worksheets will be completed for significant training events, such as PT sessions and foot marches.

RISK ASSESSMENT MATRIX

Severity		Probability Frequent A	Likely B	Occasional C	Seldom D	Unlikely E
Catastrophic	I	E	E	H	H	M
Critical	II	E	H	H	M	L
Marginal	III	H	M	M	L	L
Negligible	IV	M	L	L	L	L

E – Extremely High   H – High   M – Moderate   L – Low

COMPOSITE RISK MANAGEMENT WORKSHEET

For use of this form, see FM 5-19; the proponent agency is TRADOC.

1. MSN/TASK	2a. DTG BEGIN	2b. DTG END	3. DATE PREPARED (YYYYMMDD)

4. PREPARED BY

a. LAST NAME	b. RANK	c. POSITION

5. SUBTASK	6. HAZARDS	7. INITIAL RISK LEVEL	8. CONTROLS	9. RESIDUAL RISK LEVEL	10. HOW TO IMPLEMENT	11. HOW TO SUPERVISE (WHO)	12. WAS CONTROL EFFECTIVE?

Additional space for entries in items 5 through 11 is provided on Page 2.

13. OVERALL RISK LEVEL AFTER CONTROLS ARE IMPLEMENTED (Check one)
☐ LOW   ☐ MODERATE   ☐ HIGH   ☐ EXTREMELY HIGH

14. RISK DECISION AUTHORITY

a. LAST NAME	b. RANK	c. DUTY POSITION	d. SIGNATURE

DA FORM 7566, APR 2005

ITEMS 5 THROUGH 12 CONTINUED:							
5. SUBTASK	6. HAZARDS	7. INITIAL RISK LEVEL	8. CONTROLS	9. RESIDUAL RISK LEVEL	10. HOW TO IMPLEMENT	11. HOW TO SUPERVISE (WHO)	12. WAS CONTROL EFFECTIVE?

DA FORM 7566, APR 2005

Made in United States
Orlando, FL
20 January 2023

28861214R00028